TENSION AND CONFLICT IN NORTH -EAST INDIA

TENSION AND CONFLICT IN NORTH -EAST INDIA

by

KUMAR

COSMO PUBLICATIONS
2015 New Delhi

TENSION AND CONFLICT IN NORTH-EAST INDIA

Cosmo Publications
This COSMO Print 2015

ISBN: 81-7020-862-0

Published by
COSMO PUBLICATIONS Div. of
GENESIS PUBLISHING PVT. LTD.
24-B, Ansari Road, Darya Ganj,
New Delhi-110 002, INDIA
Ph.: 2327 8779, 2328 0455

Dedicated

To The

Memory Of

Professor Umashankar Joshi

Contents

Preface

The tension and conflict in North-East India is due to the intersection of diverse social, political and economic forces. The strong-hold of colonial history, Indology, anthropology on our elite, creating obsessions, the real and imaginary grievances in the name of identity crisis have contributed to the present situation.

The paper on "Language Politics" by Professor V.V. Rao was published in the Thinker edited by me. The papers on "Autonomy movement in Naga Hills District" by Prof. S.K. Barpujari were presented in a seminar organised by me at Tuensang. These papers come under the parameter of the theme and are included in the present volume.

I shall feel rewarded if the book contributes to the generation of positive thinking on tension and conflict in the region.

B. B. Kumar

Acknowledgements

The author gratefully acknowledge the help rendered by Professor V. V. Rao and Professor S. K. Barapujari for their papers included in this volume.

1

Tension And Conflict In North-East India

Tension and conflict is not new to North-East India. Soon after the formation of Assam as a Chief Commissioner's Province in 1874, Sylhet was added to it on 12 September 1874. This started the politics of tension between the Assamese and Bengalis. There was conflict of interest, and language politics generating grudges against each other. There were attempts to annul the amalgamation, sometimes by Hindus and sometimes by Muslims of *Borak Valley*; sometimes by the Hindus of both valleys. However, Sylhet continued to be part of Assam till the dawn of independence, when a part of the district was merged with East Pakistan (now Bangladesh). The dominance of the people of *Borak Valley* in Assam affairs and their opposition to the cause of the setting up of Gauhati University and Gauhati. High Court in preference to Calcutta University and Calcutta High Court, sharpened the differences between the two valleys.

The problem of immigration of Bengali Muslims in the Brahmaputra Valley became acute from the early part of this century. The Line system, which was introduced to safeguard the interests of the Assamese was often violated and immigrants many times grabbed land by fraud. The Assamese, without much caring for their future, sold their lands as the immigrants often offered exorbitant prices.

The problem of immigration became acute as early

as 1931 and a note of caution was voiced in the 1931 census report about the situation to be faced by Assamese and their identity every where except in Sibsagar district. The problem did not surface after independence as the Bengali Muslims tried to hide their identity by declaring Assamese as their mother tongue in the census reports. However, when twenty eight Muslim MLAs were elected in 1978 elections and names of 7500 foreigners were detected in Mangaldai parliamentary constituency, it led to the six year long agitation against the foreigners spear-headed by the All Assam Students Union, All Assam Gana Sangram Parishad, Assam Jatiyatavadi Dal, Purbanchaliya Loka Parishad and Assam Sahitya Sabha. This region has witnessed a many faceted conflict between the states and different ethnic groups. There are border conflicts between states and conflict as well as violent clashes between different groups in every state. Autonomy demands by various groups continue to plague the region.

The ethnic hatred often takes the shape of communal outbursts. The assertion of identify often takes negative turns such as in agitations against Assamese and Bengali Scripts and ban on use of *sari* by Tripuris.

The present social tension in North-Eastern India is due to the interaction of the diverse historical, social, political and economic forces. Neither are the factors generating of these forces new to the North-Eastern situation, nor the forces which have emerged. In the present situation these forces which were dormant for some time, have only reappeared with their new permutations and combinations, creating an explosive situation. The forces operating in the North-Eastern scene are a strange combination of both integrationist and disintegrationist, constructive and destructive forces. The movement, if we take the entire region into consideration, has an adequate share of violence and non-violence. The tragedy is that in the present situation, the forces, which are so vigorously active in the North-Eastern scene are thoroughly successful in dividing our people into two camps. The picture which is painted day and night is either perfectly white or perfectly black. An atmosphere charged with emotions, distrust and fear is created knowingly as well as unknowingly, making it impossible for the voice of dissent to be heard and thereby widening the gulf. A hysteria is successfully built up, which needs urgent remedy, so that reason has its effective appeal, the rigid attitudes smoothen and national leadership gets time to diffuse and solve the problem. Unfortunately, even those who are supposed to be highly responsible persons and who ought to refrain from expressing such tendentious reflections as are likely to exacerbate relations between different communities, are failing to do so.

The present social tension in this region poses a complex problem before the nation. There is a need for imaginativeness and thorough understanding of the situation, which may be utilised with patience, determination, ingenuity and tact, to find a solution that benefits the region without harming the country. It is really very difficult to take a holistic and balanced view of the complex situation specially when widespread attempts to create confusion, distrust and bias are being made; but there is hardly any way out. This is necessary for abandoning rigidity and for the creation of goodwill, which is so vital and essential for any negotiated settlement of the problem. The North-Eastern situation demands the strongest possible political will to make it apolitical, a will to view it as a purely national problem.

It will be a grave mistake to regard the present massive agitation and unrest in North-Eastern India as accidental. It is also not the effect of a sudden cause. Both, the tendencies of confusing effect for cause and to view it as an accidental and sudden phenomenon are clearly visible, which are bound to result in misjudgement and dangerous consequences.

As already stated, many factors are responsible for the present state of affairs in North-Eastern India, some of which are given below:-

Demographic Factors

1. *The changing demographic pattern* in some of the states of North-Eastern India has been the greatest cause of unrest in this region. Overall growth rate of population in Assam was as high as 34.97% and 34.95% for 1951-61 and 1961-71 respectively which was higher than all-India rates (21% and 24.75% respectively) during the same period. The increase of population from 55.61 lakh in 1951 to 145.25 lakh in 1971 was remarkably high. In the case of Tripura the rate of population increase was the highest. This was certainly due to large-scale influx of population from Bangladesh and Nepal. The Assamese, who are continuing their nine-month old movement for the detection of foreign nationals, their defranchisement and subsequent deportation, term this large-scale influx as a "silent invasion". They apprehend a threat to their language and culture if this influx is allowed to continue. The case of Tripura and Sikkim is cited in this regard, where the original settlers were swamped and outnumbered by the large influx of immigrants. The movement run by All Assam Students Union (AASU) and Gana Sangram Parishad (GSP) is also supported by Assam Sahitya Sabha, which is giving it an intellectual flavour. The movement received the present intensity and momentum after the Lok Sabha polls in 12 constituencies of Assam and Meghalaya were postponed. The spontaneous fervour of the movement supported by the masses, is certainly also due to fear of being outnumbered.

While immigration is not a new phenomenon for this region, its massive nature from the beginning of this century is new for Assam and other neighbouring areas. This region has seen planned large scale immigration of tea-garden labour from far away places like Bihar, Orissa, U.P and Andhra, by British tea planters followed by large-scale planned Muslim immigration from East Bengal (specially from Mymansingh District) by Sadulla's Muslim League Ministry in pre-partition days. This was done with a view to including Assam in East Pakistan.

Lord Curzon, the then Viceroy of India, divided Bengal into two parts on communal lines to pursue his policy of divide and rule. He tagged Assam, without any justification, on to the Muslim majority East Bengal Province. This initiated large-scale influx of land hungry peasants from highly populated East Bengal districts. Here it may be recalled that Assam which was once a highly populated, well developed region of the country became highly depopulated, during the last century due to the repeated Burmese invasions. The devastation caused by the invasions was so great that many areas of Assam during the course of half a century were converted into dense forests. It took hardly fifty years for the highly inhabited Dhansiri valley to be converted into the famous Nambor forest (the densest forest of Asia). The same was the case of Kapili valley in Nowgong district which has the largest concentrations of such immigrants. The immigrants, who came to Assam in the early parts of this century, occupied the forest reserves, waste lands and *chor* areas. Cases of forcible occupation of the patta lands were also reported. The famous "line system" was introduced in 1920 in Barpeta subdivision of Kamrup district and in Nowgong district to prevent such indiscriminate and illegal occupation of vast area of land by the immigrants. The line system, which barred the settlement of immigrants in certain categories of land, did not succeed in preventing immigration. this caused serious concern among the Assamese people, who protested against the inflow of lakhs of people. Their protest, however, failed to bring any result.

Very soon, the partition of Bengal was undone, but by that time the large-scale immigration was already taken to be a serious problem. As early as in 1911, the Census Commissioner warned that unchecked immigration was "likely to alter permanently the whole future of

Assam and to destroy, more severely than the Burmese invaders of 1821, the whole structure of Assamese culture and civilisation". C.S. Mullan of the Census department warned that Sibsagar would ultimately remain the only district where the Assamese race would find a home of its own. These remarks and large scale immigration created concern in the minds of the Assamese intelligentsia which slowly developed into a sense of alienation from the rest of India. As a consequence, even persons like Nilmoni Phukan joined Ambikagiri Roy Choudhury in representing to Jawaharlal Nehru that, as a means of saving the Assamese race from extinction, a considerable section of the Assamese intelligentsia had even expressed views in favour of the secession of Assam from India.

The pace of immigration increased after independence. Post independence immigrants fall into the following three categories:- (a) Hindu refugees from East Pakistan (now Bangladesh), (b) Illegal Muslim infiltrators from East Pakistan and (c) Immigrants from Nepal. The case of former two categories should not be mixed up. Unfortunately such tendencies abundantly visible, are creating a lot of confusion and apprehension. Again, the cases of the Nepalis of Indian origin and those who came to India from Nepal recently are not alike and the latter should not expect the same treatment.

Let us examine these cases separately.

Partition of India and the Refugee Problem

The devastating effect of the partition of the country is most felt in the eastern sector. One of the most important sections of our pre-partition population, whose contributions and sacrifices for the freedom of this country were second to none, overnight found themselves third grade citizens of a hostile country. Freedom, which was once so dear to them, became a curse; the day of independence was the beginning of an unending nightmare. Millions left their home and hearth for an unknown destiny, only to experience untold suffering. More than forty seven years have passed since that day but their sufferings are yet to end and the human flow from across the borders is yet to cease. About ten million victims of the 'Two-Nation Theory' are still residing in Bangladesh. They are there in a state of perpetual terror with swords hanging over their unfortunate heads. Who will guarantee them their freedom and safety?

It is true that next to West Bengal, Assam and Tripura have received the largest number of refugees from Bangladesh. Their continuous influx has undoubtedly created demographic imbalance and therefore needs to be checked. The refugees who have come to India, fall into the following categories:

(a) Registered naturalised persons: they are Indian citizens with a right to stay anywhere in India.

(b) Refugees who came to India earlier but due to ignorance or any other reason have not registered themselves as Indian citizens; but who are otherwise living a settled life. Such persons should be awarded Indian citizenship. They should not be forced to leave their home and hearth a second time.

(c) Refugees who came to India earlier but due to their ignorance or otherwise have not registered themselves as Indian citizens; and who are yet to be rehabilitated. A section of this category of persons may be taken out from Assam and settled in other states.

(d) The refugees coming to India after the cut off period, should be deported back to Bangladesh.

In the last instance, some pertinent questions emerge. Should India deport these persons to Bangladesh without adequately safeguarding their rehabilitation and safety there? What can we do if Bangladesh does not agree to take them back? What can this country do to ensure safety for the minorities of Bangladesh? (Reports are pouring in about fresh atrocities on Chittagong Buddhist tribals by Bangladesh armed forces. The tribal population constituted 97% for the population of these hills before partition) . If atrocities on the minorities of Bangladesh are not stopped, then will they not try to cross the boundary and come to India?

India was a party to the creation of the history of partition and therefore cannot escape the resultant responsibilities. For India, to demand adequate safeguards for the interest of the minorities of Bangladesh, is a part of its moral responsibility thrust on it by history. It cannot be denied by India on the pretext that it will mean interference in the internal affairs of Bangladesh. If India protests loudly for the cause of Palestinian refugees without interfering in the internal affairs of Israel, there is no reason why this country's protests cannot be louder for the cause of the refugees in India and for the ten million minorities of Bangladesh, who may otherwise be forced to come to India as refugees later on. Needless to say, India can hardly afford to receive them, as that will defeat all its family planning efforts and shatter its economy.

Problem of large-scale illegal infiltration

Large-scale, unchecked infiltration of foreign nationals from Bangladesh started right after the independence. This further disturbed the demographic pattern of this region, which had to shoulder the responsibility of the rehabilitation of millions of refugees coming from that country. Immigration from Nepal provided yet another dimension of this already complicated problem.

The provisions of the Immigrants (Expulsion from Assam) Act, 1950, could not be implemented due to certain difficulties. Shri Bishnu Ram Medhi, the then Chief Minister of Assam, wanted to implement it and he persuaded the Central government to make certain amendments so as to tide over certain difficulties; but he was removed from Chief Ministership soon after that.

The news of Pakistan flags being hoisted in parts of

Assam during the period of Chinese aggression in 1962 caused concern throughout the country. The Consultative Committee of Parliament for Home Affairs made some recommendations in this regard. Shri B. N. Mallick (the then director, C.I.B.) was also sent to Assam to investigate into the matter. The members of the Consultative Committee were informed in an informal meeting by the Home Minister, Shri Lal Bahadur Shastri, that the Central Government had agreed to take measures to check the inflow of illegal entrants into Assam from across the borders, as short-term and long-term measures, and some of the measures were: increasing the number of border outposts and check-posts, strengthening the existing check-posts and delegation of full powers under the Foreigners Act, 1946, to the Superintendents of Police and District Magistrates in the border district for summary deportation of Pakistani infiltrators.

The Central Home Minister visited Assam for about a week during the early part of 1954 and announced certain measures for the deportation of illegal infiltrators. The announcements made by the Home Minister were welcomed by the Assam Pradesh Congress Committee, which adopted a resolution on 1st April, 1964 in which some practical measures were also suggested. Some of the relevant parts of the resolution are quoted below:

"The problem of Pakistani infiltrants is posing a serious problem for the security of this frontier State. The Committee welcomes the various announcements made by the Union Home Minister after about a week's visit to Assam on the question of expeditious deportation of illegal infiltrants.

"The Committee also feels concerned about the reports of harbouring infiltrants in some areas. The committee will like to make it clear that such anti-national activities call for stringent measures against the offenders. In the interests of the security and peace in the State, it is very necessary that every man should extend his full co-operation in tackling this problem. The Committee, therefore, appeals to the people of Assam to extend their full cooperation to the administration in detecting such illegal infiltrants.

"Strict vigilance is necessary on the part of the people."

The following concrete steps were suggested in the resolution:

(i) That a target date not later than March 1965 to complete the deportation of Pak infiltrants in Assam be announced and acted upon accordingly.

(ii) That the Citizen's National Register with house number intended for preparation of the Census of 1951 be made the basis of tracing out Pakistani nationals and deporting them without delay.

(iii) That adequate number of tribunals be appointed immediately to achieve complete deportation of Pakistani nationals within the target date.

(iv) That a strip of land with such depth as may be needed along the entire East Pakistan border be cleared of all habitations and declared a "prohibited area."

Soon after, in the year 1964, a scheme known as the "Prevention of infiltration of Pakistanis into Assam" (PIP) or Nehru scheme was put into field operation. The scheme was drawn up by the Assam Police and financed by the Central government till 1969. Several quasi-judicial tribunals were set up for the purpose. The scheme was often opposed by certain circles; but Pandit Nehru firmly backed it. Some M.Ps from Assam made a representation to Pandit Nehru in 1962 against the scheme, to which he replied: "It is time infiltration was stopped and effectively dealt with. Therefore, steps have been taken recently to stop such infiltration. We may take further steps to remove illegal immigrants and we may fix 1952 as the date of our enquiry."

The tribunals functioned effectively without political

interference upto 1967. The immigrants were given an opportunity to establish their claim to Indian citizenship in the light of the Citizenship Act, 1955, and other related enactments and 1952 was taken as the base year for the purpose. During 1964-1969, 2,40,000 infiltrators were detected, of which 1,92,000 were deported. Only 20,000 cases could be decided during the period 1967-69, as against 32,000 in 1963, 72000 in 1964, 73,000 in 1965 and 25,000 in 1966. After 1967, political interference started and the scheme was ultimately dropped in 1969. It was again revived by the Assam government on 4th October, 1979; but it is yet to start functioning. The controversy over the cut-off year should be settled for its re-functioning.

The Nehru-Liaquat Ali Pact, India-Mujib Pact, and constitutional and legal provisions regarding foreign nationals should provide three dimensions for any consideration and the things should be decided soon in the perspective of greater national and regional interest so that the tribunals once again start functioning without any let-up and hindrance.

Large-scale, post-independence, illegal infiltration of foreign nationals was made possible mainly due to (i) mismanagement of forest reserves and other government lands in North-Eastern India. (ii) loose international borders and (iii) harbouring and shielding the illegal infiltrants by a section of people.

(i) Mismanagement of forest reserve land and other government waste-land: anybody, who has extensively toured in North-East India, knows that these lands provided readymade shelter for lakhs of illegal infiltrators. This was not possible without the co-operation of the government officials. It will be better if immediate steps are taken in this connection.

(ii) Loose international borders: our difficulties are also due to our loose international borders with

Bangladesh. The above mentioned Nehru Scheme (authored by Bhola Nath Mallick, the then Special Director of C.I.B; also known as Mallick Scheme), apart from suggesting the prevention and deportation of illegal infiltration also suggested the following measures:

(a) Erection of a wall on the India and East Pakistan (now Bangladesh) border as in the case of East and West Berlin.

(b) Providing identity cards with photos to the Indian citizens residing in the Assam-East Pakistan border areas.

(c) Increasing the number of check posts on the border and intensification of border security.

Pandit Nehru, it is said, instructed B. P. Chaliha, the then Chief Minister of Assam to start the construction of the wall. The Central government was to finance the project. Chaliha unfortunately advised against the erection of the wall and the scheme was dropped.

BSF played a very insignificant role in the matter of the detection of infiltrators. In the sixties, when more than two lakh infiltrators were detected by Assam Police in a period of 4-5 years, BSF could hardly detect more than an average of 200 per year. In a recent new report, an interview with a BSF officer was published which gave a very grim picture of their ability to check influx, even during the coming two years in spite of the new arrangements envisaged. The steps taken until now to check further infiltration cannot be said to be satisfactory in spite of the old agitation continuing as before.

In this respect, it is essential to prepare and implement a co-ordinated plan on influx without any delay. Construction of walls with barbed wires, electric fencing, creation of no-man's land on the border and intensification of guarding by security personnels are essential throughout Indo-Bangladesh border. This should include West Bengal-Bangladesh sector of the border also, otherwise infiltration through that sector of the border cannot be ruled out.

(iii) It is alleged that a section of the people harbour and shield the illegal infiltrants due to obvious reasons. This not only helps illegal infiltration, but also makes their detection difficult and creates bad blood between the different communities. It is also often alleged that illegal infiltration takes place with active connivance of a section of Indian citizens, politicians, and police. A strict watch on such elements is essential. Rules should be framed in such a way that they may be firmly dealt with.

2. *State re-organisation* on linguistic lines gave momentum to the ethnic politics in North-Eastern India, which was responsible for the creation of many states and Union territories in this region and the consequent dismemberment of Assam. It had the following effects:

(a) Limiting the job-opportunities of the Assamese people.

(b) Creating a sense of deprivation in the minds of Assamese people.

(c) Strengthening of the regional and ethnic sentiments in North-Eastern India.

These factors contributed their part in generating tension in this region.

3. *Lack of understanding between the dominant communities:* i.e., the Assamese and the Bengalis in Assam, Khasis and Bengalis in Meghalaya, is not a new phenomenon. The two Bengal *kheda* movements in Assam and a few riots in Shillong created deep distrust in the minds of the people and scars, difficult to heal. Some of the reasons of the lack of understanding between the dominant communities residing in this region are the following:

(a) Over-emphasis on certain uncharitable prejudices,

like "Bengalis have superiority complex". "Assamese are idle people" etc. Such utterances need to be discouraged by one and all.

(b) Deliberate attempt to create communal and linguistic disharmony by a section of people for their own selfish and anti-national purposes.

(c) Over-play of ethnic and parochial sentiments with a view to creating a sense of alienation among the various sections of the people.

Apart from the above mentioned factors there are other reasons also on which some light is thrown in the succeeding chapters.

4. *Faith in the effectiveness of agitational methods:* In recent past, there was mass agitation and *satyagraha* by the Assamese people for : (a)the bifurcation of North-Eastern Railway to form North-East Frontier Railway, (b)location of head quarters of N. F. Railway in Assam, (c) building of the first road-cum-rail bridge over the Brahmaputra near Gauhati, (d) demand of a second bridge over the Brahmaputra near Tejpur, (e) providing a broad-gauge railway link upto Gauhati, (f) construction of a mini-refinery at Noonmati (Gauhati), (g) a bigger refinery at Bongaigaon, (h)recognition of Assamese as the State language, and so on. A community, which has to take recourse to agitational methods to get the tiniest of their grievances redressed, cannot be blamed for their faith in the effectiveness of agitational methods.

The stiff attitude of the Assamese people during the present agitation is partly due to their faith in the effectiveness of the agitational methods and partly due to their lack of faith in the present State-mechanics.

5. *A wrong belief in a section of the people that "violence pays",* leading to insurgent activities: Insurgency by Mizo-rebels in the early sixties and

the latest insurgent activities in Manipur (first by Kuki-Chin insurgent groups, later on by Pre-Pak, people's Revolutionary Party of Kungleipak, and MNF: Meitei National Force) and Tripura (by extremist Tripura Upajati Juba Samiti, Tripura, National Volunteer Force and Tripura Sena) should not be labelled as mere misadventures on their part.

6. *Unimaginative Bureaucracy:* If there is a general belief in a large section of the people of this region that agitation and recurring violence may ensure a massive flow of resources from New Delhi, then the lion's share of the blame must go to the unimaginativeness of the bureaucracy. It is necessary to ascertain how and to what extent this factor is responsible for misdirectional and disproportionate growth of primary sector, wrong plan and development priorities leading to the lack of adequate infrastructure and transport facilities, perpetuating a sense of backwardness and neglect and lack of industrialisation in this region.

7. *It needs a thorough study as to how far the apathy,* short-sightedness and selfish motives of the ruling elites including all shades of politicians are responsible for aggravating the problem in the North-Eastern region.

8. *Bottleneck psychology:* A very narrow land-mass (only, few kilometers wide near Siliguri) links this region with the rest of the country. This has added a new psychological factor. Due to this bottleneck psychology, this region needs constant reminding that the rest of the country has no apathy towards this region and due attention is paid to their defence and other needs.

9. *Overemphasis on certain historical facts:* In this region, certain historical facts are unnecessarily overemphasised and unnecessarily repeated in

public utterances and writings. These take the form of allegations and counter-allegations and create an atmosphere of mutual distrust and fear.

"Indian leadership", barring Mahatma Gandhi, is charged with having agreed to a proposal of a formula of Cripps Mission according to which Assam was to be grouped together with the Muslim majority East Bengal to form a Muslim majority State. The people revolted against this plan under the leadership of Shri Gopi Nath Bordoloi, who was helped by Mahatma Gandhi.

On the other hand, it is argued that the partition of Bengal was the result of the fear complex and rigid posture of the Assamese leadership, which sealed the fate of undivided India and of the Bengali Hindus. Indian leadership wanted to give a cautious trial to the Cabinet Mission plan so as to bypass the vexed communal question and consequent partition of Assam. Undivided Bengal and Assam were given almost evenly balanced representation in the constitution-making. Assam was also empowered to opt out from Section C if it so desired. The AICC resolution gave a clearcut assurance that "it will not compel Assam to act against the declared wish of the people through the Legislative Assembly". But all the persuasions, explanations and even AICC resolution failed to allay the apprehensions of the Assam leadership. It is also alleged that Assam leadership unnecessarily agreed to divide Sylhet district of Assam to get rid of the Bengalis.

It is also often repeated that Nehru abandoned the people of Assam in the face of the Chinese aggression. The allegation, although not true, has a wide appeal due to the bottleneck psychology of the people and provides enough ground for harbouring a grudge against the national leadership. The truth is that Nehru (like any other Indian leader or member of the public) was exceedingly disturbed and distressed by the military reverses suffered by India in Wallong, Sela pass and Bomdilla on November 18, 1962. It was necessary for the Prime Minister of a country to reassure its people on such occasions. Nehru, accordingly in a radio broadcast, appreciated the feelings of the friends in Assam and pledged that India would not only extend all help to them to its utmost ability but also continue to fight and drive the Chinese away from the Indian soil.

It is often repeated that Bengalis wanted to impose their language on Assamese people. This is too old a phenomenon which is disproportionately publicised and unnecessarily gives an opportunity to a section of Assamese people to sharpen their grudge against a section of their own fellow Indians. In this context it is necessary to remember that the Britishers themselves introduced the Bengali language in Assam in the early part of their annexation of Assam (as they did in other parts of Bengal Presidency) for administrative purposes. Assam did not have an adequate number of people knowing Persian or English at that time, therefore, it was not possible to introduce these languages for administration of that State as was done elsewhere in those days.

10. *Distortion of historical facts:* Deliberate attempts to distort history have become a regular phenomenon in this part of the country. Unfortunately, the academic community is fully participating in this foul game. This helps the upsurge of all sorts of chauvinism. A fuller study of this topic, although of a controversial nature, will be highly interesting and paying in terms of national integration.

11. *Failures of the academic community:* The academic community in this country is imitative rather than creative. This is more so in the case of North-East India, and mostly in the field of social sciences. Most of the works published in the name of research are mere crude descriptions of people, society, and events. They lack reasoning and analysis. They are full of quotations from the writings of British officers, without judging the authenticity of what they wrote. The fact that they were pioneers

in the field does not undermine a more important fact that they were not trained academicians (anthropologists, historians, etc) and what they wrote was not without bias. The *Matsya Nyaya* period (a period of anarchy) continued in this region for a fairly long time, which affected the observation and judgement of the British writers, who lacked a deeper understanding of everything which was Indian. Unfortunately, everything which is written and published in the English language (and specially so if written by an individual with a white skin) has a seal of authenticity for the Indian elite.

Most of these writings describe the minutest of our differences, ignoring the massive, apparent as well as hidden similarities. In this way, they tend to boost regional and ethnic sentiments. The instances of crude generalisations and over-simplification are numerous. In the North-Eastern context, studies about what the nation and the national leadership have done for the betterment of the living conditions of the people and all-round development of this region are mysteriously few. Needless to say that such studies are absolutely necessary for creating goodwill and for national integration. On the other hand, the minutest lapses are magnified to create a sense of alienation and permanent grudge.

It is found that often the situation is allowed to deteriorate and when it takes a serious turn and explodes, then third rate academicians rush with their crude theories and explanations mainly to attract the attention of persons sitting in the corridors of power (as they believe that power and power alone can get them recognised) . In this way they not only tend to degenerate into a third rate protective mechanism around the establishment (the protective mechanism which the establishment needs no more), but also by doing so, they confuse the nation and thereby cause delay tackling the problem which consequently brings a series of shocks due to the chain of repetition of such events.

Hundreds were butchered in Tripura not because the people of Tripura, Jamatias, Halams and Reangs were strangers to the Indo-Aryan ethics and they were forced to conform to the values of the Ganga Valley's ruling class. A poor cobbler sitting on the footpath of Thangal *bazar* to earn his butterless bread and a *pan* shopkeeper of Paona *bazar* with his worries for not being able to purchase medicine for his ailing wife had certainly done nothing to prevent the recognition of Manipuri language as a language of Eight Schedule of the Constitution. The reason for the mad fury, causing arson, killing and mass evacuation are certainly not so simple. A university teacher of Jawaharlal Nehru University is meak, timid and clever enough not to assert that the old Manipuri script was also of Indian origin and its replacement should not cause a grudge against the nation as a whole. Similarly he does not contradict the false propaganda that Mainipuris were converted from animism to Hinduism by King Garib Niwaz. He is the last man to come in the way of reassertion of Meithei nationalism. Then why should he be harassed and assaulted?

The academic community has always let this country down during crises. It lacks calibre, devotion, professional morality and courage of conviction (of course it does not have any conviction) to say what the ruling elite should be told rather than what they want to hear. This community is highly conscious of its privileges, comforts and promotions. It unnecessarily suffers from fear psychosis of being kicked in the stomach. This makes them dogmatic rather than pragmatic. A nation in crisis needs a philosophy of action which our intellectuals and academicians are incapable of providing.

The failure of the academic community in the present context (as in any other crisis of the post independence era, be it economic, social, political or due to external aggression or internal instability) does irreparable harm to the nation, mostly in three ways:

(a) It fails in its duty of providing clearcut guide-lines for proper and timely action.

(b) It confuses the nation and helps in delaying the solution of the problem and causes misuse of scarce resources and

(c) It dampens the spirit and the will of the nation to fight against the odds.

North-East India has four universities (including an agriculture university) and an university centre (J.N.U. Centre at Imphal). The academic achievements of these universities, apart from providing degress in prototype courses and thereby helping in the creation of an army of the unemployed and subsequently adding to the problems of society are insignificant. Some of them are as yet non starters in this respect. Hectic academic activities divert the attention of the students towards the finer values of life and help in easing tension. It creates a congenial climate for mutual trust, understanding and creativity.

12. *Yellow Journalism:* The social tension in North-East India is also due to yellow poison generously injected into its body.

13. *Communication gap:* There exists a wide communication gap between this region and the rest of the country. Wrong policies are adopted due to the ignorance of the politicians and administrators. Many newspaper editors and intellectuals, academicians, and columnists, write on this region without visiting it even once and with only a very shallow knowledge of the region. Factual errors, sweeping and generalising remarks, tendency to explain everything so as to fit into a preconceived ideological framework and motivational trend of analysis become too obvious when one glances through the flood of articles written in bad taste, which are published in our newspapers and magazines. This

attempt of mass education by those who themselves need education, further aggravates the problem of an already existing communication gap.

The knowledge of our intellectuals about this region is so poor that even the difference between the Assamese (Asomiya, Ahomiya) and Ahom is safely forgotten. Statements like, "Ahomiyas who themselves came from China. . . ", ". . . many Ahoms might justifiably feel they are in danger of being swamped", ". . . 20 million North-Eastern Mongoloids. . . ", "Nagas live in Golaghat district of Assam. . . " appearing in the editorials and columns of national dailies clearly indicate the utter ignorance of our information about this region. Here, I would like to quote a few lines from an editorial of a national daily newspaper. It says, " Behind the agitation and posturing by its sponsors, and the talk of keeping illegal immigrants out of the voters' list lies the unmentioned question, whether Assam should exclusively be for the Assamese speaking people and all those who speak any other language, should be kept out of the voters list even if they have lived in Assam for generations. This is not only an entirely unreasonable demand but also unconstitutional. It questions the very foundations of the Indian republic". Some pertinent questions may be asked here- What are the constitutional rights of the illegal immigrants? In what way does illegal immigration help in strengthening the foundations of the Indian republic ? Who, according to the editor, are illegal immigrants?" It is clear that the editor has failed to understand and differentiate between the illegal immigrants and non - Assamese speaking Indian citizens of Assam. All this creates confusion and also helps in generating a sense of insecurity in the minds of non-Assamese Indian citizens of Assam and thereby helps in creating tension.

14. *Political misapprehensions:* A demand was made in 1954 before the State Reorganisation Commission to include Goalpara district of Assam in West Bengal. A similar demand was made to form a full

fledged state comprising of Cachar district of Assam and Tripura (it was only a class C state) at that time. This demand was made on the plea of these areas being predominantly Bengali speaking. It created misunderstandings between the two dominant communities of Assam. The demand of "*Brihattar Bangla*" from certain circles further aggravated their fear and misapprehensions. There was a slight tilt in the linguistic representation in the Legislative Assemblies of Assam, Meghalaya and Manipur during the last Assembly elections, which did not go unnoticed. A regional party named Purvachal Rajya Parishad by Abdul Kadir Laskar, was formed with the aim of the creation of a separate Bengali speaking state named "Purvachal" out of Assam. The party declared its intention to fight elections in ten parliamentary constituencies of Assam. This also generated psychological tension.

15. *Explosion of aspirations of the youth:* There was a rapid expansion of the educational facilities in this region in the post independence era. Similarly, due to the increase in the number of states, and expansion of administrative machinery, employment opportunities increased manifold. This catalysed the explosion of the aspirations of the youth of this region. The revenue-earning productivity and industrialisation was, however, slow and the employment potential of the administrative machinery has reached its saturation point. Thus there is a potential source of strain and tension.

16. *Vested interest in keeping up social tension:* A section of the society in this region has developed vested interest in keeping up social tension due to various reasons.

17. *Secessionist forces:* It is not a secret that secessionist forces are active in this region. We

have read about Sula (Seven units liberation army) and many other such organisations. Such forces become ineffective in an atmosphere of mutual trust and understanding. These forces endeavour to create discord, misunderstanding and deep-rooted distrust between the various communities. With their well-knit propaganda machinery they try to strengthen the parochial tendencies and help in sharpening the deep rooted sense of grudge and mass-resentment by constantly telling the masses that they are exploited. The tone of the slogans written on the walls of many North Indian cities and towns needs careful study. They convey the message to the dominant communities that they are being exploited by the outsiders. They also convey a message that their language and script are being neglected. This is no way different from what was done in North-East India sometime ago. Posters saying that 'Assam, gives oil, etc., and gets only salt' is a part of an organised game. The meak, mild, well behaved and hospitable Tripuris were constantly told that they were exploited by the outsiders and that nothing is done to develop Kok-Barak (Tripuri language) . Same was done in Manipur and elsewhere in this region. The poison worked slowly, unnoticed by the short sighted leadership. Slowly a community became organised and aggressive, and others terror-stricken and panicky. Other methods like killing a man here, another there, some cases of arson and looting, underground literature and notices threatening one community or another were also used for creating a sense of insecurity, specially in the minds of non-dominant communities. The slogans raised against the Bahiragat (people coming from other states of India to Assam) in newspapers of Assam created suspicion in the minds of non-Assamese Indian citizens of Assam. This helped in creating confusion between the illegal immigrants, refugees and non-Assamese speaking Indian settlers.

These elements also try to extend the area of conflict and thrive on genuine mass grievances without which it is difficult to create an explosive situation. Once such an explosive situation is created, the reason becomes the first casualty and it becomes very easy to spark a stir. "Trigger-happy CRP men sparked Manipur stir" was a newspaper caption. It is found that many clashes between different communities of this region were sparked by individual fights. This shows that upsurge of parochialism has created an explosive situation.

What happened in Manipur and Tripura recently was perhaps an experiment to find out the effectiveness of mass terror as a means of large scale reshuffle of population. It should be our endeavour to see that the same is not repeated elsewhere. This seems to be the second phase of their technique, which, if allowed unabated will start the third phase i.e., the chain reaction of such events elsewhere and thereby undermine the basic concepts of our republic.

At a time, it is necessary to rehabilitate the people involved in secessionist activities, but it should not be made a routine affair so that the lure of the unemployed youth to get employed and rehabilitated through violence becomes great. The V.I.P. treatment by passing through the corridors of violence sets a tempting precedence.

18. *Foreign hand:* It is alleged that active foreign hand is operating behind the scenes and helping the turmoil in North-East India. China and Pakistan actively supported insurgency in this region. The reports of training camps for Tripura tribal insurgents operating in Bangladesh are too fresh in our memory. The help rendered by other countries in creating tension in this region is also reported from time to time. The question is why should these foreign countries help anti national activi-

ties in this region and what do they want to achieve in this way. It is not difficult to find an answer to these questions. These countries with the help of anti national elements and their collaborators may try to convert this area into a region of instability, with a view to bringing a third split in this sub-continent. The centripetal forces i.e. nationalist forces in this region were always stronger than the centrifugal ones. It is necessary to have a balanced view of the situation and not to overemphasize and exaggerate the strength of the latter.

Action needed

The present situation in North-East India demands early and firm action on the part of central leadership. The people of this region should be made to believe that Government understands their problems and is sincerely trying to solve them.

It is necessary to solve the foreign nationals problem for ever, by sealing the borders with Bangladesh (by creating a no man's land and laying mines if necessary). The reports of Assamese-medium mobile schools in Bangladesh point to the fact that they mean to continue the influx of population to this country. A study of the demographic change in the border villages in certain sectors due to acts of the criminals from across the border is also necessary.

While sealing the international border, it is necessary to ensure diplomatically that minorities in Bangladesh are allowed to live safely.

It is also necessary to remove the genuine hurdles in the way of the development of this region.

2

Aspects of History and Historical Background

North-East India comprises of the States of Assam, Manipur, Meghalaya, Nagaland and Tripura, Arunachal Pradesh and Mizoram. These seven states have a total area of 2,59,054 sq. kms., which is approximately 8% of the total geographical area of the country. It is inhabited by about three crore people mostly tribal. Except for the three valleys, namely, Brahmaputra Valley, Surma (Barak) Valley and Imphal Valley, the remaining two-thirds of the area of this region is hilly.

North-Eastern India has attracted considerable attention of the people of this country as well as that of foreign countries due to various reasons. This region has witnessed armed insurgency which was aided directly or indirectly by China and Pakistan now Bangladesh. This generated much concern in the minds of the people of our country, as this area has strategic international borders. It borders China (Tibet) in the north, Burma in the east and south-east and Bangladesh in the south and south-west. The principle of state reorganisation based on linguistic lines was successfully challenged in North-Eastern India and as a result, the formation of states like Meghalaya, Manipur and Nagaland took place. However, there were other factors also which contributed towards the formation of these states. This diversion in the principle followed in the formation of States on the lines other than the linguistic one gave a new dimension to the history of post-independent India.

Assam was famous in the whole of India as a land of magic and witchcraft. The temple of Kamakhya in Gauhati is one of the most sacred Shakta Hindu Shrines. The fact that Assam has contributed most in the Tantric development of Hinduism and Buddhism, is accepted by one and all. The genesis of such a development will give us a clue to understanding the process of fusion of races into one Indian race and ideas which are basically Indian. One point which I would like to emhasise here is that the area where such a fusion took place did not end in the Brahmaputra valley, but extended hundreds of miles further north, north-east, and south-east. The Bon religion of Tibet, a strange combination of Shaivism and Shaktism according to the Himalayan Gazetter was already well established in Tibet when Budhism entered. The fact that the Bon religion continued to give a determined fight to Buddhism upto the recent past, specially in south-east Tibet, clearly indicates that it was an established and ancient religion at the time of the entry of Buddhism in that country. For the proper assessment of the process of Indianization, these extended frontiers of Indian history, both in area and time, should be kept in view. It is necessary to note that although India ends at its political boundaries, the Indian phenomenon does not allow shrinking of political boundaries.

The Europeans pioneered the work of writing the history of the North-Eastern region. " A History of Assam" written by E. A. Gait, is one of the monumental works in this direction. While we appreciate the pioneering works of the foreign scholars, it is difficult to ignore the distortion and over simplification of facts in their works. Although it is difficult to analyse such distortions and over- simplifications in brief, nevertheless, I would like to mention some of them.

The Europeans failed to depict the history of North-Eastern region in a proper perspective due to many reasons. The conditions prevailing at the time of their entry into this region was also partly responsible. The early period of British rule in Assam was a period of anarchy (what is known as *Matsya-Nyaya* period in India political terminology). Vast areas, which were like gardens a few decades ago, were depopulated and in the process gradually converted into densest forests. In the words of E.A. Gait, "The conditions of Brahmaputra valley at the time of expulsion of the Burmese was most deplorable. No less than thirty thousand Assamese had been taken away as slaves, and a well known native authority was of the opinion that the invaders by their barbarous and inhuman conduct had destroyed more than one-half of the population which had already been thinned by internecine commotions and repeated civil wars. Those who survived had been so harassed by the long continued wars and repeated acts of oppression that they had almost given up cultivation and lived chiefly on jungle roots and plants. Famine and pestilence carried off thousands that had escaped the sword and captivity. Thc Ahom nobles and the great Gosains, with a few exceptions had retired to Goalpara, after losing the whole or the bulk of their property, and they were followed by a large number of the common people. The former eventually returned to their homes but the poorer refugees did not, and their descendants still form a large proportion of the inhabitants of Goalpara.

This movement of population was not only in one direction, but towards all the directions to the neighbouring hills. Valleys of the Kopili and Dhansiri rivers were once the most populated regions in the North-East. They were depopulated in no time. What was once the garden-like, well populated, well cultivated valley of Dhansiri, became the densest forest of Nambar in the course of a few decades. According to Mr. Gait, "the Burmese... in revenge for the friendly disposition which the Assamese had shown towards the British troops pillaged all the surrounding country and committed appalling atrocities on helpless inhabitants. Some they flayed alive, others they burnt in oil, and others again they drove in crowds into the village Namghars, or prayer house which they then set on fire".

"The terror which they inspired among the people was so great that many thousands fled into the hills and jungles... where large numbers died of disease or starvation; and only a small remnant, after enduring unspeakable hardships managed to reach the plains of the Surma valley. Several of the sub- montane villages of Jaintia are inhabited by their descendants, who still talk pure Assamese. The depopulation of the region around Doboka and the Kopili valley dates from this disastrous time, which is still fresh in the minds of the inhabitants of Nowgong, who speak with as much horror of the Mahar Upadrab or "oppression of the Burmese".

During the early part of British rule, Singphos and other Himalayan tribes attacked the plains of Assam and took thousands of people as salves. The raids of the hill people on the plains continued till the end of the last century. Raids and counter-raids by and among the hill people and punitive expeditions by the Government, were regular features of British rule in North-Eastern India in the nineteenth century. Needless to say, this gave a bias in their historical viewpoint and they were unable to assess the real power and authority enjoyed by the kings of Assam over the neighbouring hill areas.

The state of affairs in North-Eastern India in the nineteenth century was an exceptional one in the whole history of this region. A comparatively longer period of dynastic rule of the kings of this region was only possible if they did not face the same challenge from the neighbouring hill tribes, as the Ahoms faced in the last part of their rule and the Britishers in the beginning of their rule in this region. Long dynastic rule in a narrow strip of land like the Valley of Brahmaputra or that of Imphal and Burma could only be possible if there was an understanding and harmony in power equations between the people of hills and plains of North-East India.

Dearth of early historical records is an all-India phenomenon. Naturally, like the prehistory of the rest of the country, the history of the North-Eastern region of that period is also based on gleanings from a few ancient inscriptions. There are copious references of *pragjyotish* in *Mahabharat* and *Kamrupa* in *Puranas* and *Tantras*. *Kalika Puran, Vishnu Puran* and *Yogini Tantra* give the boundary of Kamrupa in the ancient times, which does not show any exaggeration over that of the Chinese Buddhist pilgrim, Huen-tsang, who visited India in the first half of the seventh century and also Kamrupa during that period during the reign of Bhaskar Varman (600-648 A. D.) Huen-tsang says that the circumference of the kingdom of Kamrupa was nearly 1, 700 miles and its western boundary was the Karatoya river, while the eastern boundary was a line of hills adjacent to the tribes on the Chinese frontier.

One point, which deserves mention here, is that the political system in this part of the country was similar to that of the rest of the country. Like other parts of the country, this region had local chieftains under the petty kings who in turn accepted the sovereignty of the monarch. Bhagdatta, the legendary king of *pragjyotish* and Bhaskar Varman, the king in the seventh century accepted the overall sovereignty of the central authority i.e. Yudhisthir of the *Mahabharata* age and Harsha, the India monarch of the seventh century respectively. The horse-sacrifice (*Ashwamedha-Yajna*) was also performed by the Varman kings of Kamrupa, such as Mahendravarman, Bhutivarman and Sthitvarman and their imperial powers were duly recognised.

India allowed decentralization of political power with limited control by the monarch. The boundaries shifted, but India remained India. A look at the following quotation from the *Sutra of the Excellent Golden Light* shall make my point clear.

"When the eighty four thousand kings of the eighty four thousand states are contented with their own territories, they will not attack one another or raise mutual strife. When all these kings think of their mutual welfare and feel mutual affection and joy, contented in their own dominions, India will be prosperous, well-fed, pleasant and populous. The earth will be fertile, and the months and seasons and years will all occur at proper time. . . And all living beings will be rich with all manner of riches and corn, very prosperous but not covetous".

The decentralized political power frame provided a strong and effective control mechanism at the grass-root level, strength to the system and relative stability inspite of wars and occasional strife. This system successfully worked till Turk and Afghan invaders with a different political philosophy attacked India and tried to destabilize it. The conscious readers of Indian history fully understand the need of a strong and united India as the external threat with its manifestations shall always remain. Under the umbrella of a strong central power, we need to have effective decentralization of power upto the lowest level.

This should operate in a democratic frame. The grass-root democracy should not function under a conflict situation where unity is always at stake and the whole society is divided. Consensus should guide the working of democracy to avoid wastage of energy. Unfortunately, this has not happened and this is one of the sources of tensions in society in North-East India and the rest of the country. In conformity with the above mentioned political philosophy, India has always had democracy at the grass-root level, and regional and sub-regional rulers with different degrees of political control. North-East India was no exception.

The foreign invasion posed a threat for traditional Indian polity and the traditional ruling elite. However, very soon the invaders learnt to live and co-operate with the system and to use it for their benefit. Akbar used the system and stabilized Moghul rule in India, Aurangzeb countered it and as a consequence the Moghul empire became weak. The British smoothened their rule in India as they used the existing control mechanism to their advantage. The Nagas, who had fought them tooth and nail, cooperated with them and a single Deputy Commissioner could ensure satisfactory law and order situation. We undermined the system and made it ineffective and could not fill the void by creating a monolithic, huge law and order machinery. As a result, there is violence and disorder everywhere. This statement is valid for the entire country, but more so for the tribal areas of this region.

The hill people of North-Eastern India and those of the Himalayas were termed as Kiratas. The fact that Ganges and goddess Durga are termed *"Kirati"* stands in the way of accepting it as a racial connotation rather than a geographical one.

North-Eastern India has immense linguistic, cultural, social and religious diversity. Inspite of the apparent diversity in view, there exist a large number of factors which unite the people of this region with each other on the one hand and with that of the rest of the country on the other. A study of the various aspects of life, beliefs, and folklore of the various communities of this region will reveal the unity in diversity (rather, the diversity in unity), which is certainly the outcome of centuries of contact and the process of give and take it generated. Except for a few cases, clan endogamy is prohibited throughout the country including the tribal areas of North-Eastern region. The concept of a supreme being which is the Creator, but not worshiped as He is uninvolved in the after affairs of creation, is shared by the people through out the country. Most of our languages have the "subject-object-verb" pattern of sentence. These are a few examples only which illustrate the age old contact and common shared heritage of the Indian people.

The myth of race was given undue importance by the Britishers, as it helped their imperial ends. They tried to forget that the people of this region have a thorough mixing of bloods. In this connection, I would like to refer two points; Firstly, Indian society was not fussy about purity of Blood. this may be proved by copious examples from Vedic, Epic and Buddhist literature. The mother of Vyas, the editor of Vedas and the *Mahabharata* was a fisher-woman. The same woman, Satyavati was the ancestress of the *Kaurawas* and *Pandavas* of epic fame Hypergamy and caste mobility had social sanction to a great extent. This is more true in the North-East region. Social degradation by declaration as *Vratya* and restoration of status by *Vratya-stom* were both permissible, allowing two way mobility. There are numerous examples of caste—tribe continuum and spatial mobility. Secondly, the society worked for cohesion and integration. In caste-society, a community found a place in *Varnas* frame. In tribal society, the distinct and diverse ethnic elements were gradually integrated. The dominant trend was towards perfect homogeneity. The social and not the ethnic frame was, and still continues to be dominant. It brings homogeneity. At best there is superimposition of one on another with a perfect equation to allow social harmony. Ethnic diversity used to exist only temporarily. A non-Chang in a Chang village and a non-Tangkhul in a Tangkhul village were essentially sub merging their identities. Among Limbus (also known as Kiratis or Kirantis) of Libuan region of Nepal and western Sikkim, almost half of the clans are known as *Kasi gotra* and another half as *Lhasha gotra*. The tribe allowed two distinct ethnic groups to merge their identities into a single homogeneous identity. Thus the entire social mechanic worked for cohesion, harmony and homogeneity and not for the neterogeneity and divided identity. Anybody else in a tribal village was to be adopted by a clan of that village to be an integral part of the same.

Apart from strengthening the myth of race, British colonialists also over-emphasised the migration of races and the migration theory. The British were the latest in coming to India and perhaps they wanted to convey to the Indians, "You came yesterday and we came today. The country either belongs to you and to us or to none"

For them the vast fertile enchanting and loving land mass of India — tenderly loving as a mother, was just empty till Aryans, Dravidians, Mundas and Indo-Mongoloids came to people it just a few thousand years ago. India with all the gifts of nature, sun-shine, rivers, abundant water, fertile soil, hospitable climate etc. had the curse of remaining empty. Central Asia and North Europe with all the anger and fury of nature and devoid of natures gifts were the cradles of civilization: humanity flourished where nature was hostile. The illogical theory of migration has been carried to an absurd end by colonical masters.

The study of castes and tribes was started by our colonial rulers, resulting in publications of many beautiful and scholarly monographs. The study of Indian culture, religions, languages etc. was a welcome development. 'Linguistic Survey of India' by G.A. Grierson was a monumental work. While studying the language of the then *Madhya Bharat*, a team going from the Hindi area described it as a dialect of Marathi and another team coming from the Marathi language side claimed the same language to be a dialect of Hindi. It is clear that the dialect has something in common with Hindi and Marathi both, but the emphasis of the study was on pointing out the differences, rather than on similarities. The aim of the studies of the colonial master was to depict India as a confused and divided entity. This was a part of a well laid out strategy prepared after the 1857 sepoy mutiny. The micro studies on castes and tribes and other such work depicted India as a heterogeneous and confused conglomeration of different races, cities, tribes, languages, dialects, regions, and religions. They were successful in projecting the empire as the liberator, the deliverer of good, the unifier of India and the best guarantee for safeguarding the interests of the fringe areas, the tribals and the untouchables. "Descriptive Ethnology of Bengal" by Dalton, and numerous monographs by Gurdon, Lyall, Johnstone, Hutton, Mills, Shakespeare and others were written by in pursuance of the policy framed by Alfred

Lyall who was an important colonial functionary. They provide valuable information and many of them are true masterpieces. There was a need of macro studies based on such works and massive field and library works by Indian writers.

The search of the hidden cord of unity within Indian society by scholarly and objective studies by scholars to break the trend set by followers of Lyall was essential for India. Unfortunately, the trend set by him continues, and macro studies have failed to replace micro studies. The academic community and its culture of hundred quotes and re-quotes have not only failed to answer the imaginary conflict situation of core vs fringe, Aryans vs non-Aryans, exploiters vs exploited, caste vs tribe, giver vs taker etc. but have strengthened the same. Gait gave a strange twist to the history of Assam based on the fact that (1) the early kings of Assam had *Asura* epithet and therefore, they were non-Aryans and (2) the river names of Assam start with the syllable *Di* (Boro word for water) and therefore the land belonged to them. The word Asura had behavioural connotations and therefore *"Vritraghna"* (Killer of Vritra i.e., Indra) of Rigveda was also *Brahmaghna* (Killer of Brahmana) and *Vritra* was both *Asura* and a Brahmin. The word *di* and similar words in Mizo etc. are in no way different from the word *"toya"* for water in Sanskrit. *Garibniwaj* was instrumental in replacing one sect of *Vaishnavism* with another. Meitheis were Vaishnavites before him and remained Vashnaivite after him. This fact is ignored and a distorted history is presented to the readers. History of North East India is full of such oversimplifications and distortions which send wrong signals and strengthen the assumed grievances.

The regional sentiments based on the dichotomy of core vs fringe are mainly based on misgivings. They need academic answers more than anything else - as in reality, the said dichotomy is a myth. The problems and sufferings, the dreams and aspirations of the tolling masses, the peasants and tribals are the same everywhere. The peasant and tribal societies operate on the same wavelengths. In case of languages, inspite of linguistic diversity, India is a language zone. These facts need to be conveyed in a proper perspective to the people to generate a deep sense of belonging. The communication gap needs to be bridged. Many parts of India such as the North East fringe of Bihar remained unconquered by the Moghuls, but the people of those areas never made issue out of the fact as is done in the North East. I take it as a failure of our academic community, which is incapable of answering them at the level of ideas. Basically, our academicians are the consumers and not producers. This is why our academic disciplines, specially history, anthropology, indology, sociology and linguistic continue to be colonial disciplines. The various obsessions of academicians and their lack of commitment further complicate the matter. India was facing the problem of insurgency in Nagaland, but Shrinivas did not care to cross even Tista, leave aside the Brahmaputra, for the study of social change in this part of the country. The works of Roy Burman are mostly descriptive. Indian historians, with the exception of Tapan Ray Choudhary and Irfan Habib, did not care to study the history of the North East as a part of the history of India. Even Roy Choudhary and Habib included the history of the medieval period of Assam only in the Appendix of the Cambridge History of India Vol 1 (1982). Serious studies on North-Eastern language are lacking, and for many, Grierson stands on the boundary of frontiers of knowledge. The study of politics and state systems needs to be done in a pan Indian frame. The analysis of the trends, the processes, the systems and the frame in such studies are more important.

The central government has generously given funds for the development of the region and yet there is a massive grudge. The political elites of the states are more responsible than anybody else for the silent demographic aggression by Bangladesh, but the anger is directed elsewhere. The leaders of the anti-migration movement of Assam performed daecimally when given the power to rule and act. There is a massive systems failure. The problem of Bangladeshi Hindu refugees was to be tackled diplomatically, but India miserably failed in doing so and claiming proportionate land from Bangladesh. In reality, we have lauded the case of Palestinian refugees more than that of our own. Similarly, the problem of illegal immigration of Bangladeshi Muslims is a national problem, but our obsession with religion has forced us to close our eyes towards communalisation of the same.

A large number of our problems are based on assumed grievances of an academic nature and therefore need academic answers. Unfortunately, our academics have failed us in such cases.

3

The Identity Problem and Its Expression

The various communities identify themselves by their respective names. In many cases, the name given by the community for itself differs from that given by its neighbours. In the course of time, old names are invariably replaced by new ones.

Generic names are usually given to a cluster of communities especially when their distinction is hazy or if less is known about them by the community which gives a name. Few decades ago, Assamese used to say 'Bangal' to everybody coming from the West, irrespective of whether they are Bengalis or not. Similarly, Manipuris called everybody *'mayang'*. It may be noted that the words "Bangal" and *"mayang"* originally denoted the inhabitants of Bangal and Cachar respectively.

The identity of a community is a changing phenomenon. Sometimes smaller identities get submerged in a bigger one. Naga identity formation out of two dozen different tribal identities is an example of greater identity formation. Prior to the advent of the British no Naga tribe was calling itself 'Naga'. Now every tribe identifies itself by that term.

The British used to call all non-Naga tribes of Manipur *Kuki*. Sometimes the generic term *'Kuki-Chin'* was also used for them. The term is more used today for denoting their ethnic and linguistic unity. After independence, a new tendency was seen among *'Kuki-Chin'* tribes of Manipur whereby they started claiming their separate clan identities as their tribal identities. Thus the reverse phenomenon of parochialization in identity formation which may also be called 'smaller identity formation' emerged. However, this phenomenon is not seen among the *Kuki-Chin* tribes of Mizoram and Nagaland. In Mizoram, which was called Lushai Hills after the name of the dominant Lushai clan, all the *Kuki-Chin* tribes like Mizo, Paite, Hmar, Zou, Kom, Thadou etc. prefer to call them Mizo. There was a rift between the Thadou clansmen of Manipur and Nagaland. While in Manipur they call them Thadou Kuki, in Nagaland they simply call them Kuki.

A phenomenon of shifting the identity is also withnessed. Anals of Manipur speak a *Kuki-Chin* dialect. Dr. Grierson in his linguistic survey has classified their dialect in the *Kuki-Chin* group and in all the old records, they were called a *Kuki-Chin* tribe. However, they claim themselves as a Naga tribe nowadays.

In olden days, every village in the hills was practically a republic. The formation of the states and union territories is also a new phenomenon, which has provided basis for a new identity, for instance a Meghalayan or Arunachali identity.

Thus we find that identity formation is a dynamic and changing phenomenon, which depends on various socio cultural and political factors. A group of tribes may develop a sense of belonging due to some common social or political experience and thereby may develop a new enlarged identity. On the contrary, a clan or a tribe may develop its own political or social vested interest and thereby may develop itself into a new tribe, resulting in parochialization. Political importance of a group may bring new affiliations to it resulting in shifting of identity.

Peasantization, tribalization and caste formation in Indian society was the most democratic phenomenon where none was prevented from claiming a separate identity. The same is true even now. No community in this country is forced to merge its identity into another. However, we hear such phrases as 'identity crisis' nowadays.

Every individual and community is free in India to claim its identity and pursue its own way of life. Nobody stops anybody from pursuing the old religion and culture or even to adopt a new one. Thus identity problem is an internal problem of a community. But whenever there is a cry for safeguarding the identity and the slogan of 'identity crisis' is raised, it gives a feeling that the problem is of exclusive nature.

The reason for this may be found in the political aspirations of the elite groups. It needs thorough and detailed investigation whether the various elite groups view the problem of 'identity crisis' in its socio-cultura parameters. If so, what is their contribution in the fields of literature, culture, development of languages etc. in their respective areas. Why are the demands of statehood always linked up with that of separate identity? Why in some cases, does the same community speaking the same language, claim separate statehood rather than asking for merger of their areas? Is it not true that the slogan of 'identity crisis' by small groups is simply raised for political ends? These problems need thorough and in-depth investigation and searching analysis.

Claiming a new state for every small area and tribe has become a fashion in North-East India. The reality often ignored is that many districts of the country are far more backward in every respect than any part of this region. They should also get their share of development. A country, like a mother, should care equally for all of her children.

Expressions of Identity

The identity problem of various communities of North-East India finds its expression mostly in political terms ranging from secession, state/union territory demand, to District Council formation. These expressions found their fulfilment in the formation of Nagaland, Meghalaya,

Mizoram, Manipur and Tripura and the formation of new District councils in Manipur, Tripura and Mizoram.

It is sad that the urge of identity assertion has failed to give impetu to creative writing and hectic cultural activities. The creative and literary activities are mostly seen in Manipuri, Khasi, Mizo, and Angani languages but not in any other language and area.

Political Parties and Pressure Groups

North East India has seen rise and fall of large number of regional political parties and interest groups in comparison with any other part of the country. These parties and groups give expression to legitimate and non-legitimate aspirations, demands, and needs of various regional and ethnic groups. Information about some of the parties and groups of the kind is given below.

(i) *Sarbadal*: Muhammad Saadulla, Surendranath Buragoha and P. M. Sarvan representing minority groups such as Muslims, Ahoms and tea-garden labour, commonly known as Bengali *coolies* were its founder co-presidents. The first two left it soon after. P.M. Sarvan continued to run it in order to look after the interests of the tea-garden labour community. After its dissolution in 1966, it was replaced by the Assam Labour Party.

(ii) *The Cachar Progressive Party*: It was formed in 1966 to protect the legitimate interests of the Cachar district, and was a very short lived one.

(iii) *Assam Gana Parishad*: After six long years of Assam agitation an accord, popularly known as Assam accord was signed on 15 August 1985. Two months later Assam Gana Parishad i.e., A.G.P. was formed as a regional political party. Two regional parties, namely, Purbanchaliya Loka Parishad and Assam Jatiyatabadi Dal and All Assam Gana San-gram Parishad merged to form the A.G.P. It came to power in 1985 Assam election. Later on there was a rift between Prafulla Kumar Mahanta and Bhrigu Kumar Phukan, There was a split in the party and Natun Assam Gana Parishad was born.

(iv) *United Minorities Front:* It was born in November 1985 to fight elections against Pro-Assam accord forces. Jamiat Ulema-e-Hind, Citizen Right Preservation Committee and the Minority Forum combined to form it.

(v) *Plains Tribals council of Assam:* PTCA was formed in 1967 for fighting for the autonomy of the tribal areas of the Assam plains. It also shared power during the Janata regime.

(vi) *The East India Tribal Union:* It was formed in December 1952 in a meeting called by Capt. Sangma. Its aim was the formation of an East Indian tribal state. Later on it was renamed as East India Tribal Union or E.I.T.U. It demanded the amendment of the sixth Schedule to the Indian constitution and grant of greater autonomy to the district councils. It also aimed at establishment of separate state comprising of the entire tribal area of North East India. It shared power in the Chaliha government. on insistence of Pt. Nehru, but left the government. on Assamese state language issue and joined the All Party Hill Leaders Conference i. e. A.P.H.L.C..

(vii) *All Party Hill Leader Conference :* A conference of the hill leaders of all the political parties of Assam (except that of Naga Hills which was called NHTA by then) was called on 6 July 1960 by Capt. W.A. Sangma to oppose the declaration of Assamese as the state language of Assam on 7th July 1960. The conference decided to convert itself into a political party. All the members of all the parties of the autonomous hill districts were its members. All the M.Ps., M.L.As. Chief Executive members of the district councils and some other from the hills were the members of the Council of Action. The

A.P.H.L.C. was instrumental in the formation of Meghalaya state.

(viii) *The Hill State Peoples Demand Party* : The party was formed after a split in A.P.H.L.C. after the declaration of the formation of the autonomous state of Meghalaya within Assam by Union Home Minister on 14th May 1968. The rebels suspected that moderates among the party accepted the autonomous state plan unconditionally and therefore separated.

(ix) *The Mizo Union* : It was the first political party in Mizoram, which was formed on 9 April, 1956. Mizoram (then known as Lushai Hills district) was an excluded area without representation in State and Central Legislatures. Mizos had autocratic chiefs. The district administration was run by the superintendent who was both the head of civil and police departments. The Mizo Union wanted to fight against such irritants. It promised the people their representation in state and central legislature, improvement of their economic and social conditions and over and above, the abolition of chieftainship. The party later on split into Mizo Union and Mizo Union Right wing. Mizo Union joined INC. A splinter group kept their separate entity.

Mizo Union earlier joined A.P.H.L.C. and promised Hills State formation. The party was also party responsible for the outbreak of rebellion.

(x) *The United Mizo Freedom Organization* : The U.M.F.O. was established by Lalmawai, a discharged Army person, who joined Burmese civil service. He wanted separation of Mizo areas and its merger with Burma. After Lalmawai's disillusionment with the Burmese, he joined East India Tribal Union and the party was dissolved.

(xi) *The Mizo National Front or M.N.F.* : Famines take

place at regular intervals of fifty years in Mizoram, when bamboo flowers and rats multiply. The Mizos knew in 1959 that there would be famines and warned the government of Assam. However, the Chaliha government failed to pay adequate attention, resulting in starvation deaths and immense suffering for the people. The people were very angry with the Assam government. They started the Mizo National Famine Front M.N.F.F. and the Mizo cultural society which were the fore-runners of M.N.F. The M.N.F. with its wing, Mizo National Army fought for secession of Mizo Hills from India.

Laldenga was the founder president of M.N.F. He was a primary school teacher, then a Havildar clerk during World War II and an accountant in the district council office after 1952. He resigned his last post as there was charge of misappropriation of district council funds. He was a fine and forceful orator.

There was deep rooted dissatisfaction in Mizo Hills against Assam government due to their mishandling of famine relief and massive unemployment due to lack of development work. The Mizo chiefs got good compensation but could not properly use the fund and became paupers and dissatisfied. The men of Second Assam Battalion who were discharged without proper rehabilitation and employment joined M.N.F. Mr. Chaliha believed the promises of M.N.F that they would remain non violent, while in reality, they were collecting arms and ammunition and in fact he pampered it to weaken M.U. Over and above, Pakistan was helping them. All these factors strengthened M.N.F and it was encouraged to resort to armed rebellion, resulting in capture of Aizawl and Lunglei on 28 February, 1966 and 5 March, 1966. Kolasib Saireng Champai etc. were captured on 3 March 66. The rebellion was short lived, but symbolic insurgency continued till statehood was given to Mizoram as a result of an agreement with Laldenga.

The number of insurgent groups, regional political

parties and pressure groups is very large in North-East India and it is difficult to write about all of them. Some of these organisations have become defunct and some are still functioning. These organisations are of three categories and some of them are listed below:-

Some of the political parties/organisations aiming at secession from India are listed below:-

1. The Naga National Council (NNC).
2. The National Socialist Council of Nagaland (NSCN).
3. The Mizo National Front (MNF).
4. The United Liberation Front of Assam (ULFA).
5. The Highlander Union, established in 1946, demanded independence for the hill areas of Assam.
6. Meitei State Committee, established in 1960.
7. United Liberation Front, ULF Manipur based.
8. United National Liberation Front UNLF; Manipur based.
9. People's Liberation Army of PIA, established in 1978, Manipur based.
10. People's Revolutionary Party of Kangleipak-Prepak; Manipur based.
11. Poilei Liberation Front, Manipur based.
12. Poilei National Army, Manipur based.
13. The Chin Liberation Army, Manipur based.
14. Legal Inspection Base of Rensak Army, Manipur based.
15. All Mongoloid Youth organisation, Manipur based.
16. The Kangleipak Communist Party, Manipur based.
17. The seven Liberation organisations for seven states.
18. Tripura Peoples Liberation Army.
19. Tripura National Volunteers.

Regional Parties

1. Assam Janata Party.
2. Karbi-A- Darbar.
3. All Assam Gana Sangram Parishad.
4. Assam Jatiatwadi Dal.
5. Purbanchal Loka Parishad.
6 Purbanchaliya Loka Parishad.
7. United Tribal Nationalist Front, working among plains tribals of Assam, specially the Boros.
8. Assam Tribal League.
9. The United Tribal Nationalist Liberation Front, UTNLF, active in plains of Assam.
10. The Manipur People's Party (MPP) .
11. The Kuki National Assembly (KNA) , active in Manipur.
12. The Manipur Hills Union.
13. The National Socialist Democratic Party.
14. The Manipur Nationalist Party.
15. The Manipur National organization.
16. All Manipur people's convention.
17. The Manipur National Union.
18. The Kanglei League in Manipur.
19. Eviebak Laishem Party, in Manipur.
20. Hill People's Conference, in Manipur.
21. The Khasi National Darbar.
22. The Jaintia Darbar.
23. The Khasi Jaintia Federated States National conference.
24. The Khasi Jaintia Political Association.
25. The Garo National Council.

26. The Hills Union.
27. The Garo National Conference.
28. United Communities Conference, UCC, in Karbi Anglong district.
29. United People Conference, UPC, in Karbi Anglong District.
30. Mikir Hills Nationalist Organisation worked for merger with Nagaland.
31. The Karbi Anglong Peoples Conference.
32. The United Karbi Liberation Organisation.
33. Mikir Hills Progressive Party.
34. Peoples Democratic Forum, PDF, Karbi Anglong based.
35. Autonomous State Demand Committee (ASDC), Karbi Anglong based.
36. The Karbi Anglong North Cachar Hill Autocad State Demand Committee (KANCHADCOM).
37. Mikir Hills Minority Party.
38. Arunachal Pradesh People's Party.
39. Naga National Organisation.
40. Naga National Democratic Party.
41. Nagaland People's Party.
42. Nagaland People Council.
43. The United Democratic Front, Nagaland based.
44. Democratic Party of Nagaland.
45. United Front, Nagaland.
46. Meghalaya United Parliament Dry Party.
47. Assam Congress.
48. Tripura Upajati Juba Samiti.
49. Tripura National Volunteers.

50. Tripura Rajya Adivasi Sangh.
51. Tripura Rajya Gana Parished.
52. Tripura Gana Mukti Parishad.
53. Tripura Rajya Gana Mukti Parished.
54. Tripura Rajya Mondal.
55. Tripura Sangh.
56. Tripura Rajya Praja Mondal
57. Assam Congress.
58. Manipur Congress.
59. Amra Bangali, Tripura based.
60. Bir Bikram Tripura Sangh, DETS, Tripura, based.
61. Cheng Crack.
62. Ujani Assam Rajya Parishad.
63. Assam Association.

Pressure Groups

1. All Assam Students Union (AASU)
2. All Assam Minorities Students Union (AAMSU)
3. The Assam Association.
4. All Bodo Students Union, ABSU.
5. Bodo Students Association.
6. The Ahom Association.
7. The Assam Sahitya Sabha.
8. Khasi Students Union.
9. Garo Students Union.
10. Pan Manipuri Youth League.
11. All Manipur Students Union, AMSU.
12. All Arunachal Pradesh Students Union.
13. Machaleima.
14. Panmyl.

15. The Vaiphei National Organisation.
16. Paite National Council.
17. Hmar National Union.
18. Gangte Tribal Union.
19. Hmar Students Union.
20. Dimasa Students Union.
21. Karbi-Riso-A-Darbar.
22. Hill State Volunteers Ad-hoc Committee.
23. Alliance for Reconstruction of Meghalaya State, ARMS, Meghalaya based students organisation.
24. Naga Students Federation, NSF,
25. Tuensang District Students Federation, TDSF. Nagaland based.

Conclusion

The list given above is in no way exhaustive. Every tribal and non-tribal group has its Students Union, mostly based on ethnicity but also location based. Their number would run into hundreds and most of them are not listed.

Political parties and pressure groups have often overlapping roles. The political roles of All Assam Student Union (AASU) and all Bodo Student Union (ABSU) in Assam agitation and Bodoland agitation respectively are well known. The roles of some regional parties in helping insurgency is also well -known.

North-East India is suffering due to an overdose of politics and the assumed identity crisis.

This is making the situation volatile, leading to unpleasant clashes, and violent outbursts. The assertion of identity is often taken to the extreme negative side such as in the case of anti Assamese/Bengali Script movements and ban on the use of *sari*.

4

Language Politics in North-East India

According to ancient Jewish legends, all mankind, at one time spoke the same language, but when the descendants of Noah tried to build a tower at Babel to reach Heaven, God became angered at their impudence and confounded their speech. Ever since, the world has been looking for a common language that will take it back to pre-Babel days.

Some like *Esperanto*, have been manufactured languages, taking the clearest, the most precise and the most easily learned roots and words, from several languages. Other have grown from a sort of international or inter-cultural baby talk into a fairly precise language with rules of grammar and nuances, all their own. Swahili is one such language which is likely to become a universal African language. It is one of the ten most spoken languages of the world and its origins are centuries old. It is a *lingua franca* of Africa, south of Sahara, and has a Bantu base and largely Arabic vocabulary.[1]

The language conflict began sometime in the second millennium B.C., perhaps between 1500 to 1200 B.C. It was at first a conflict between the two main groups, the Indo-European and the Dravidian. The Dravidian languages were in South East Asia. The Indo European languages came later on. Since 1000 B.C., the Indo-European languages have been slowly but steadily pushing back the frontiers of the Dravidian languages.

Sanskrit is the great language of the Indo-European family. Besides Sanskrit, Bengali, Gujarati, Hindi, Urdu, Marathi and Simhalese, to mention only a few, belong to this group. The Dravidian languages are Tamil, Telugu, Canarese and Malayalam. The constant advance of the Indo-European languages into the territory once occupied by the Dravidian group, was galling to the speakers of the latter. They felt that they were the victims of linguistic and cultural imperialism of the Indo-European group. When the Constituent Assembly of India adopted Hindi as the official language of the Union, the Dravidians felt that this was a manifestation of Indo-European cultural aggression, which they had been experiencing for some three centuries. When the Government of India made attempts for the greater use of Hindi in educational and administrative institutions, the resentment of the Dravidians, particularly of Tamils, flared up. The Dravida Kazhagam, under the leadership of Periyar Ramasami Naicker, went to the extent of burning the Indian Constitution and using abusive language and violence against Hindi-speaking people and also against the Aryans-the Brahmins.

There was bitter conflict in Sri Lanka between Sinhalese and Tamil. The Sinhalese said 'Sinhalese only'. The Tamil's answer to this was 'Right of secession'.

In the south, the Tamilians were afraid that their political and economic interests would be imperiled by the development of Hindi. They also feel that their inherited culture, symbolised by their own language, was being slighted. So the Madras government went to the extent of declaring Tamil not only as a state language but also as the medium of instruction even in colleges. At the same time, we may note the situation in the south is paradoxical. While the war between Tamil and Hindi is going on, Hindi is spreading like a forest fire. The number of candidates appearing for the various examinations conducted by the Dakshina Bharat Hindi Prachar Sabha is enormous. The Andhra and Mysore governments have made Hindi a compulsory subject for study in the middle and high schools.

Apart from the inter-conflict between the Indo Aryan and the Dravidian Languages, there are intra-conflicts between the members of the same group. The basis of this conflict is that people speaking the same language should, as far as possible, live in the same state. In the 19th century, the slogan was "one language, one state". This slogan was used to create new states. In the present century the slogan is "one state, one language". The implication of this slogan is that only one language should be preferred to all others for official use in the state. The result of this slogan is that there is conflict between the members of the same group. For instance, there was a conflict between Tamil and Telugu which was solved by the creation of Andhra Pradesh. There was conflict between Tamil, Canarese and Telugu. These conflicts were solved by the creation of Kerala and Karnataka (formerly Mysore) States. There was also a bitter conflict between Marathi and Gujarati and it was solved by the creation of two states, one for Gujaratis and the other for the Marathis. Later on, there was conflict between Hindi and Punjabi and it was solved by the creation of two states of Haryana and Punjab. In 1955, the language conflict assumed dangerous proportions and the integrity of the country was threatened. At present, all the major languages mentioned in the Eighth Schedule to the Indian constitution, except Urdu and Sindhi, have their home land. The language conflict is now confined to North and North East India. It is between Hindi and Urdu in Uttar Pradesh and Bengali and Nepali in North Bengal and Assamese and Bengali in Assam.

Assamese vs. Bengali

The conflict between Assamese and Bengali language began in 1847. When the Ahoms came to Assam, as invaders, they brought with them their own language. A problem arose whether they should adopt the local language or impose their own language upon the conquered. Shrewd rulers as they were, the Ahoms did not like to generate opposition to their rule in the local people by the imposition of their own language. So they adopted Assamese as the state language.

After the annexation of Assam by the British, Assamese was the language of the Courts. It was used with great "facility and convenience" and with universal satisfaction for about fifteen years from1824 to 1839 in almost every department of the public offices. Then suddenly Assamese was supplanted by Bengali for reasons best known to the rulers of the day. Perhaps the rulers of the day thought that Assamese and Bengali were one and the same language though the two languages were distinct.[3]

The cause of Assamese as the medium of instruction was taken up not by the Assamese themselves but by the American Baptist Missionaries in Assam. They brought argument and reason for the adoption of Assamese as the medium of instruction in schools. Brown, an eminent scholar of his day, described Assamese as a beautiful, simple language, differing in most respects from, rather than agreeing with Bengali. Therefore, he pleaded for the introduction of Assamese as the medium of instruction and the publication of books in Assamese. Brown wrote, "I feel persuaded, a boy will, under this system of tuition, learn more in two years than he is now acquiring in four years. An English boy is not taught Latin until he is well-grounded in English. In the same manner, the Assamese should not be taught in foreign languages until he knows his own". Thus, Brown was the single greatest benefactor of Assamese language.

On 3 March, 1847, the Commissioner of Assam wrote to the Deputy Governor of Bengal about the introduction of Assamese in Assam. The latter requested their Commissioner to procure information relating to Assamese dialect and the "degree in which it partakes of and differs from Bengali". On 14 September, 1847, the Commissioner of Assam forwarded. specimens of different dialects in use in the Province of Assam accompanied by the observation of W. Robinson relating to the connection between Assamese and Bengali languages.

In 1854, When Moffat Mill was sent by the Bengal Government to report on Assam, several representations were make demanding the introduction of Assamese as Court language and medium of instruction in schools. One of the important witnesses that appeared before the Mills Commission was Anandram Dhekiyal Phukan. Phukan argued that Assamese and Bengali were distinct from one another. He gave a list of 114 words and showed that as many as ninety had no connection whatever with Bengali."

Another witness that appeared before the Mills Commission was Danforth, who insisted that instruction in schools must be through the medium of the mother tongue. Danforth said, " We might as well think of creating love for knowledge in the minds of stupid English boys by attempting to teach him French before he knows anything of the rudiments of English. To my mind, this feature of the educational policy pursued in Assam is not only absurd but destructive of the highest motives of education and must necessarily cripple the advancement of schools as well as separate them from the sympathies of the people."

Danforth gave another reason why Assamese must be the medium of instruction. " The exact sciences should be taught in the vernacular. The teaching of these sciences is to excite inquiry, call out the reasoning powers and develop and discipline the mind. Such knowledge should, therefore, be conveyed through the most natural channels of thought so that the whole mind may be occupied, untrammeled by the medium."[6]

In 1854, Moffat Mill, while enquiring into the state of affairs of Assam, received a number of complaints against Bengali being the court language. Mill in his report on Assam observed. "The people complain and in my opinion with some reason, of the substitution of Bengali for the vernacular Assamese. Bengali is the language of the courts, not of their popular books and *shastras* and there is strong prejudice to its general use. It is because instruction is imparted to the youth in a foreign tongue that they look only to government for employment. Assamese is described by Brown, the best scholar in the Province, as a beautiful simple language, differing in more respects from than agreeing with the Bengali;and I think we made a great mistake in directing that all business should be transacted in Bengali and that the Assamese must acquire it. It is too late now to retrace our steps. But I would strongly recommend Anandram Phookan's proposition to the favourable consideration of the Council of Education, viz. the substitution of the vernacular language in lieu of Bengali, the publication of a series of popular works in the Assamese language and the completion of the course of the vernacular education in Bengali."[7]

The American Baptist Missionaries not only pleaded for the introduction of Assamese as the medium of instruction in schools, they also said that text books in Assamese should be published. When Brown and O. Cutter came to India, they brought with them a printing press. The first printing press was established by them as early as in 1836. Brown was again the first to publish in 1844, the first newspaper in Assamese-Arumoday (the Sunrise).

Again, the Christian Missionaries were the first to publish books in Assamese. The English Missionaries Carey and Marshman in collaboration with Atmaram Sarma of Kaliabor (Nowgong) translated the Bible into Assamese and published it in 1873. They were the first to write Assamese grammar and dictionaries. In 1839, W. Robinson published a grammar of the Assamese language. In 1848, Brown published his grammatical notes of the Assamese Language and Mrs. O. Cutter her vocabulary. Thus, Brown, Robinson and Nidhi Levi were the trio that stand out prominently as the founders of modern Asamese literature. They were also the founders of the movement for the restoration of Assamese to its legitimate position.

In 1862, the natives of Kamrup petitioned to the Government of Bengal that their language had not been adopted in the courts and schools.[8] The Bengal Government forwarded this petition to the Commissioner of Assam for his comment. The Commissioner observed, "I fully concur with the petitioners in their statement of the inconvenience resulting from the ignorance of their native dialect. To me, it appears certain that a native villager would not, in a court of justice, understand one word of his case, if proceedings of the case were recorded in Bengali, neither would a pure native of Bengal be able to understand the same if read out to him in Assamese although an educated Bengali or Assamese might probably be able to make out the report of the written proceedings if he had leisure to study it.".

The Commissioner also wrote that Assamese and Bengali were two different languages and therefore recommended the adoption of Assamese as the language of the court and schools in Assam.[9]

The Bengal government took three years to reply to this letter. They said, "The real difference between the two languages (if indeed Assamese can be called a separate language) is confined to a very small number of vocables and consists chiefly of inflexions and terminations. The character used both for Bengali and Assamese is one and the same, and while Bengali has considerable literature, consisting of both original works and of translations and more than one good dictionary, there is no Assamese literature except a few bald translations of elementary English Books nor anything deserving the name of a dictionary.

The Lt. Governor has been assured by you that no practical inconvenience arises from the use of Bengali in the courts as Bengali is thoroughly understood by all, who are in the habit of attending, and none is prevented from writing and presenting petitions in Assamese if he chooses to do so. All the officers of the Commissioner are required to pass in the colloquial Assamese and the *Amlahs* are nearly all natives of the Province so that no one speaking and understanding only Assamese can fail to make himself understood. Moreover, there is a considerable population in Assam, besides the hill tribes, who do not speak Assamese and barely understand it. To these people, it is a matter of indifference whether the language of the courts be Bengali or Assamese and the latter has not even the advantage of being the universally spoken language of the Province.

Under these circumstances, the Lt. Governor sees no occasion for any change in the present system and only deems it necessary to request that you will be careful that the use of Bengali does not lead to the employment of foreigners or to the exclusion of the natives of Assam from public offices for which they were otherwise eligible."

Thus, the government of Bengal rejected the petition which demanded the introduction of Assamese as the Court language and medium of instruction in schools.

But the citizens of Assam did not keep quiet. They again petitioned the Bengal Government for the introduction of Assamese both in the courts and schools. In May 1872, the Lt. Governor of Bengal, Sir George Campbell, received a number of memorials from the different parts of Assam for introduction of Assamese. The Lt. Governor asked the Commissioner of Assam for a report on this question. He wanted to know what language was spoken at home, what language was used in schools, whether a considerable proportion of the *Amlahs* of the Assam understand it, what language was spoken in each district, what language was used in courts, whether a considerable proportion of the *Amlahs* of the Assam Offices and courts were Assamese. He also wished to know whether objections to the use of Bengali were insuperable and "what reason there is for using Bengali among the Assamese people. " Sir George Campbell said, "*Prima facie*, it would seem natural to use Assamese and if we are to use Bengali, it must not only be shown that evils of the course are not intolerable but also that there is a strong reason for adopting an apparently surprising course."

At that time Assam was ruled by an extremely able commissioner, Henry Hopkinson. Hopkinson requested the Deputy Commissioner and Assistant Commissioners of the Plains districts for their opinion on the language question. He also consulted the Superintendents of Police of Kamrup and Nowgong and the Inspector of Schools.

It is interesting to note that all the district officers were not natives of Assam. They were drafted, further, from the military and had no college education and yet they dealt with this question thoroughly which no Assamese of the day was able to do. The entire correspondence relating to this question before 1874 is contained in a closely printed file which is available in the Assam Records Office. The opinions expressed by the officers are diverse, and interesting to read. The notcs prepared by Henry Hopkinson and C. N. Philip are extremely interesting. They are interesting because both of them adopted diametrically opposite attitudes. Hopkinson would condemn Assamese. Philip would advocate Assamese. We shall briefly summarise the arguments and counter arguments advanced by the officers.

The opinion expressed by the officers may be classified into two, those who were in favour of Assamese being the medium the medium of instruction and those who were in favour of Bengali being retained as the language of courts and schools. We shall consider the views of those who were in favour of Assamese. Capt. A. N. Philips, the Assistant Commissioner, North Lakhimpur, was by far the foremost advocate of Assamese as the court language and as medium of instruction in schools. He brought out very clearly and very cogently the distinction which marks and divides the two languages Assamese and Bengali throughout, "making anything like assimilation impossible."

Philip said. "I do not think that Bengali ought to be retained either as court language or as the school language in Assam for I believe the difference between it and Assamese to be wide and so essential as to make the two languages, for all practical purposes. almost as distinct from one another as are English and French. "Philip said that Bengali *Ch* becomes *S* in the hands of an Assamese. Thus *chilly* in Bengali becomes '*silly*' in Assamese, *choak* becomes *soak, chuckle*' becomes '*sukle*', '*chink*'-'*sink*' and so on.

Philips goes deeper into the question and says that in Bengali *tata prostut koria* become in

Assamese *tak jugat kori*

Again, *dibar protgyae* in Bengali become

Dibolui gatlot in Assamese.

Bengali, *Amake bhoron poshan na diwate*

Assamese, *mok pohpal mokerah*

It is not possible to quote in full what Philip said in this connection. His long note is extremely interesting. It displays that this civil servant make a thorough study of the problem.

As regards the advisability of retaining Bengali as the language of the government schools, Philip was against it. Philip contended that as long as Assamese had no dictionary and no books, this use of Bengali was a matter of necessity but now that it has both, it appears to me a distinct error in principle to allow a foreign tongue to oust the native language. Philip wrote, "I feel persuaded that an education having Bengali as the basis will never be half so popular or so much sought after by the people generally as one which accepted their mother tongue as the medium of instruction might be expected to be. If it be the object of our system to place the benefits of education within reach of the entire population, without distinction of class, I confess I cannot see the expediency of substituting a foreign language for the Assamese as the medium of instruction, unless there are very strong grounds for hoping that it would in time displace the latter altogether as the language of the country. At present, I am certain that there is not the smallest ground for such hope and I should personally regret it if there were, as I consider colloquial Assamese to be superior to colloquial Bengali in every way. . . they have (as a people and especially the better classed) too great a contempt and dislike both for the Bengali and for their language, for it ever to be possible really to convince them of the intrinsic superiority of that language over their own. When we remember that English has not even yet driven the rude Welsh vernacular out of more than a part of the small principality of Wales, it would surely be rather chimerical to expect a despised language like Bengali to supplant Assamese in Assam. . . I believe that to make Bengali the school language in the present state of things is in reality rather an obstructive than a progressive measure and opposed to general interests of the people and I think probably if Assamese were substituted, the number of our students would, before long, be doubled."

Again, Philip said that Bengali was not entitled to least favour on the ground of its supplying us with legal and technical equivalents of this kind which it has borrowed from Persian and Arabic.

Major T.Lamb, the Deputy Commissioner, Kamrup, added " The argument generally put forward is that there are so many Bengali words used by the generality of Assamese that the language must be Bengali. They may doubtless have sprung from the same root as have European languages from Latin, but no one would venture to call them the same on that account. As far as the written character, there is similarity, it must be admitted, but I submit that the articulation of sounds by means of which the natives of Assam communicate their ideas to one another are widely different to those employed by Bengalis."

One of the evils arising from what is called Bengali being the court language is that persons look to the study of that as most advantageous to them and their children in after life, and consequently the study of Assamese has been set aside to a greater extent, but the language is nevertheless spoken generally by the Assamese at their homes, in their villages, at *hats* and in fact universally, for they can speak nothing else."

"It is of primary importance", said M.O. Boyd, the Assistant Commissioner, "that the language of the courts should be intelligible to the mass of the people and therefore, that Assamese which alone fulfills this condition should take the place now held by Bengali.

"The recognition and adoption of Assamese in lieu of Bengali would be hailed with the highest satisfaction even by the better educated and more influential natives of the district as being suitable to the wants and requirements of the great bulk of the illiterate and ignorant whose cases predominate in the different courts.

"The language used should be Assamese in the courts and schools. The *pathasalas* should teach nothing but Assamese but the *zillah* schools might also teach Bengali to those who wished to learn that language. " "However similar the two languages may seem, the fact remains that if a *ryot* in the moffussil be addressed in Bengali he would not be able to understand what was said. " wrote Major A.E. Campbell, the D.C. of Sibsagar.

But the proposal to make Assamese the court language and the medium of instruction in schools was opposed by C.Cornish, the Assistant Commissioner, who said, "I am not one those who believe that any practical good would accrue from the substitution of Assamese for Bengali as the written official language of courts and government schools. . . for courts and schools of a higher grade, a technical vocabulary and terminology is required and here is the weak point in the arguments for the introduction of Assamese. It may be a distant offshoot from Sanskrit but it possesses no literature worthy of the name and no standard of the written language, We may even concede that it is as fine a language as Bengali but it has not yet passed through the stages which render a language a proper vehicle for conveying education nor has it acquired that fixedness which is required of an official language. It is at present only the tongue of a rude peasantry whose advance in civilization has been constantly checked by successive hordes of savage conqueror. "

A. Anley, the Superintendent of Police, wrote, "The language spoken by the people of Kamrup is nothing more than perverted Bengali."

J.K. Graham, D.C. of Darrang, wrote"I am much inclined to consider the movement for the introduction of Assamese in our courts as made not so much in the interest of the general run of the people as in those of that portion of them who have hopes of employment in the courts and to whom the exclusion Bengali would doubtless be a boon. Again, to reject Bengali would be to encourage the people to rely on a language having no literature of its own and thus to keep them in a manner at a standstill or it may almost be said to cause them to retrograde."

Major W.S. Larke, the Deputy Comm., Lakhimpur, wrote, "No change is advisable. All circumstances considered, Bengali as a court language and as a language used in schools, is perhaps more appropriate than Assamese."

The Inspector of Schools, C.A. Martin, said "I am inclined to believe that the language of Assam does not differ from that of Rangpur."

But the greatest opponent of Assamese was Col. Henry Hopkinson who was the Commissioner of Assam for nearly two decades. In 1865, he wrote to Sri Cecil Beadon that any attempt to improve Assamese must naturally tend to assimilate it still closer to Bengali until all traces of distinction between the two is lost.

"The supporters of the so-called Assamese language

only urge its being taught in the elementary classes but they shrink from advocating it in the higher classes for which they know it to be unsuited. The issue is therefore, confined to a very narrow point easy to disposal. Are we to teach after one method in the elementary classes, and according to another in the higher classes?"

A memorial signed by 22 Pleaders, 35 Mouzadars, 74 Mandals, 4 Gossains, 2 Dolye Bar Dawry and 1089 private men, a total 1226 persons from lower Assam, was submitted to the Lt. Governor of Bengal. The people of lower Assam protested against the order of the High Court imposing the dialect current in upper Assam "improperly designated as Assamese language". "In the courts of this Province in supersession of Bengali which has for upwards of forty years been recognised as the language of the court and adopted as the medium of instruction in the schools. The upper Assam dialect is spoken only by a small portion of the population of Assam and is altogether unimportant and meagre and its capabilities and chances to make itself the language of this entire Province are extremely limited. . . Bengali which had hitherto continued with utmost advantages to the real interests of our progress, to be the court language of Assam and which must yet continue for long years to be the medium of instruction in our schools before we can hope to prepare suitable text books. . . . It is undoubtedly a fact that in our religious and social usages we are identical with the Bengali." Thus, the petitioners requested that Bengali should be retained for a long time to come.

A. C. Campbell, Assistant Commissioner, Burpettah (Barpeta) wrote, "The result of more careful study of the matter has led to me to believe that the so-called Assamese language is deserving of even less consideration that I at one time had assigned to it, even as a colloquial dialect it possesses very few distinctive features from Bengali and as some proof of this, I may mention that traders, boatmen and others from Bengal who have never been in the Province before can immediately after arrival readily make themselves understood even in the village."

"I think the outcry against Bengali as the language of the courts and schools of Assam is not well-founded. Its use leads to no practical difficulty and any attempt to substitute the so-called Assamese language in its stead would only tend to cause very great confusion... that Suitors in courts have no difficulty in understanding the court language. As regards introducing Assamese into schools of Assam, Bengali is indispensable for the higher classes."

While forwarding these papers to the Lt. Governor of Bengal, the Commissioner of Assam, Col, Hopkinson said, "I think the outcry against Bengali is not well-founded. Its use leads to no practical difficulty and any attempt to substitute the so-called Assamese language in its stead would only tend to cause very great confusion. With one exception, all the *vakils* of my court are Assamese. . . I recently issued a circular to some of the most intelligent among them, enquiring if they met with any difficulty in carrying out their duties owing to the use of the present style of court language. All of them have replied that they have experienced no such difficulty and some of them expressed to me their fears that they would be ruined if the so-called Assamese was introduced as they did not know and would have to go to school again in their old age." The Commissioner also said that "the suitors in court had no difficulty in understanding the court language." Then the Commissioner argued." As regards introducing Assamese into schools of Assam, it is shown even by the best advocates of the dialect that Bengali is indispensable for the higher classes. The propriety therefore of teaching the boys in the elementary classes what they must to a great extent unlearn in the higher classes appear therefore questionable. In the village *pathasalas* which I have seen where books are used at all they are invariably Bengali books."

Finally, Hopkinson asserted that "an Assamese can understand Bengali and a Bengali, Assamese, it is true with some difficulty at first, but still they can understand each other. Again, an Assamese cannot express himself on certain subjects such as law, evidence and the like without adopting words and whole sentences from Bengali. Therefore, Assamese and Bengali are not distinct languages."

But Hopkinson's argument did not carry conviction with the Royal Government. The Lt. Governor in his Resolution of 19 April 1973 stated:

"No amount of argument about the derivative affinity can get over the fact clearly testified to and nowhere contradicted, that the people of Assam do not understand Bengali and that the petitions written in their name and the court proceedings are unintelligible to them, while the recent agitation proves clearly that a great majority of the Assamese wish to have their own language for the educational and court purposes.

The only real difficulty in the way of designing Assamese as the vernacular of the Province is the paucity of higher school books in the language and that difficulty is really mitigated by the fact so much dwelt upon by those who favour Bengali that a really literate person who knows one of the two languages can soon master the other. For teaching the higher classes of schools therefore, when Assamese books cannot be got, we must use Bengali school books subject to this limitation that Assamese must now be introduced into all the courts and schools of the valley districts of Assam. Bengali words may be employed for technical terms for which there is no Assamese equivalent and for which English words cannot be conveniently introduced, but for the rest, Assamese must be used *bonafide* as the court and school language of Assam.

In all primary schools, Assamese must be taught to the exclusion of Bengali also in all middle schools and in the lower and middle classes of high schools. When a class of twelve or more boys wish for it, Bengali may be separately taught to them as a language. In the upper classes of high schools, every subject in which there is an Assamese book is to be taught in Assamese; subjects in which Assamese school books do not exist can be taught either in Bengali or in English."[11]

(No. 1937 G. Education 19-4-1873 Bengali)

In accordance with this decision, Assamese was immediately introduced in the courts but its introduction in the schools was delayed on the ground that proper text books in Assamese were not available in adequate numbers. The Government offered handsome rewards for the production of text books. Fifty eight authors submitted manuscripts for approval. But the Commissioner refused to accept any one of them as they contained Bengali words. Hopkinson said, "I can no more get any document without Bengali than Shylock could get his pound of flesh without blood."

On 14 February 1874, C. A. Martin[12] (Officiating Inspector of Schools, Assam circle, Home, Feb 1874.) informed the Chief Commissioner that there were no suitable text books in the Assamese language on the subjects prescribed for the Vernacular Scholarships examination and sought his permission to use Bengali books in the middle schools till suitable text books were produced in Assamese language. But the Chief Commissioner replied that in Primary classes Assamese should be taught as the vernacular and not Bengali. If the boy understands Bengali better than Assamese, the teaching of the vernacular, which in primary schools will be to great extent oral may be carried on in that language. In regard to subjects other than the vernacular language taught in primary and middle classes, the instruction should be conveyed in the language the boys best understood. If the boys understand Bengali the Chief Commissioner has no objection to Bengali books being used.

Keatinge's order roused the fears of the Assamese. They thought that attempts were being made by Bengalis to supplant Assamese. There were protests and the Chief Commissioner was requested to retain Assamese in the courts and schools of Assam.[13] The Chief Commissioner assured the petitioners that there were no grounds to entertain a fear that Assamese was being supplanted. At the same time he said that Bengali would be retained temporarily in the middle classes until suitable text books in Assamese were available.

In 1897, Col. Gurdon took the initiative and introduced Assamese as the medium of instruction in some of the middle schools in Kamrup. But Bengali continued to be used in the schools. On 16 January 1903, the Chief Commissioner enquired why Bengali and not Assamese was taught in Gauhati and Barpeta High Schools. The D.P.I. replied that Sir Henry Cotton was averse to the substitution of Assamese text books in the place of Bengali text books in the High Schools of Assam Valley. Further, in Gauhati, Bengali text books were used because there was an influential Bengali community theirin and education had to be provided for their children in Bengali. It is true that in Gauhati, there was an unaided high school chiefly attended by Assamese pupils but the headmaster was a Bengali. On 28 March 1903, the Chief Commissioner desired that students in Kamrup district should be taught in their vernacular. But Dr. Booth, the DPI, thought that it would be undesirable if not impossible to implement the Chief Commissioner's suggestion. But Gurdon, the D.C. of Kamrup, wrote to the DPI on 10 April 1903, that Kamrup was an Assamese-speaking district where 83 percent of the population according to the 1901 census spoke Assamese. It would therefore, be anomalous that instruction in High Schools should be in any language other than Assamese.

On 5 March 1903, Manik Chandra Barua represented to Col. Gurdon that the medium of instruction in the High Schools in Kamrup should be Assamese. Kamrup was never a part of Bengal and that Gauhati was essentially an Assamese town. Therefore, the medium of instruction should be in Assamese and not in Bengali. P.G. Melitus, the Commissioner of the Assam Valley, supported Manik Chandra Barua and at the same time said that arrangements should be made in Gauhati to provide instruction in Bengali for Bengali boys if their parents insisted on this. Melitus thought that the feeling of a large and intelligent section of the Bengalis should be taken into account. But in Goalpara, Melitus said that instruction must be Bengali because Goalpara people had far more dealing with the people of Bengal than with the Assamese.

Melitus concluded by saying that in giving instruction in Assamese instead of in Bengali we are sacrificing efficiency. I have no doubt that better education can be given through the medium of Bengali and my experience of the Assamese leads me to doubt whether the expectation of the Chief Commissioner that suitable text books will speedily be written if there is a demand for them will be justified by the results. At any rate the Assamese text books will probably be inferior to those which will be available in Bengali. However, the sentiments of the people are entitled to some consideration.

Melitus's views were supported by the D. C. of Goalpara, and A.H.Cumming. Cumming wrote that it would be far better that Assamese language should cease to exist and that Bengali should take its place. I am inclined to think that for the present, Assamese may be the medium of instruction in middle schools in the districts where Assamese is spoken but that Bengali should be the medium of instruction in districts where it is the language of the common people. I would urge that for a really thorough education thorough knowledge of Bengali is necessary. Assamese has practically no literature of its own, ancient or modern. It possesses no newspaper on scientific works and no modern literature of any kind. I am not aware that there is a single drama or novel in Assamese while in Bengali there are many and Bengali possesses a very large scientific literature.

Although Assamese was declared as a court language and as the medium of instruction in schools and although it was included as one of the recognised languages, Assamese was not declared as an official language. The demand for the declaration of Assamese as the official language of the State was made by Assam Sahitya Sabha since 1950.

On March 3,1960, answering a question in the Legislative Assembly, the Chief Minister said "The government has not taken a decision on the subject yet. I would, however, mention that government has not underestimated its importance or the request that has been made by the Assam Sahitya Sabha and other institutions for the declaration of Assamese as the State Language. I highly appreciate the zeal and enthusiasm with which the demand for the declaration of Assamese as the State Language has been made, more particularly by the Assamese-speaking section of our population. Government would prefer to wait till they get the same demand from the non-Assamese-speaking population for the declaration of Assamese as a State language. Government feel that this question should be judged from more than only the point of view of majority or minority. If this issue is decided only on the basis of majority or minority, Government is afraid that its subject would not be decided" (AICEP 3 March, 1980). Speech of Bimala Prasad Chaliha (pp. 49-50).

There was a mixed reception to this statement. The people of Cachar district hailed this statement as that of a statesman. The people of Brahmaputra valley called Chaliha as pro-Bengali. The Assam Pradesh Congress Committee recommended to the Government that while Assamese should be made the official language, there should be no imposition whatever on the non-Assamese districts. Accordingly on 23 June 1960, the Chief Minister announced that Official Language Bill would be introduced in the Assembly more or less on the lines indicated by the APCC. This statement also had a mixed reception. While the people of Brahmaputra Valley generally welcomed the statement, the people of Cachar and some of the Hill districts resented the statement and opposed the proposal. There was near anarchy in the State. Several thousands became refugees in their own State and several were killed. Private and public property was damaged to a considerable extent. In this situation, the Assam Official Language Bill was introduced on 10 October, 1960. It received the assent of the Governor and passed into Act XXXIII of 1960.

The Act declared Assamese as the official language while English, until replaced by Hindi would be used in the secretariat and in the offices of the heads of the departments. There would be no imposition of Assamese on the non-Assamese-speaking population. All the languages which were in use in the Autonomous Hill districts would continue to be used upto the district level unless the regional or the district councils decided otherwise. Bengali would continue in the district of Cachar unless the Mohkumah Parishad, and the Municipal Boards of the district in a joint meeting by a majority of not less than two-thirds of the members present and voting, decide in favour of adoption of the official language. It also provided that all ordinances promulgated under Article 213 of the Constitution of India, all Acts, passed by the State Legislature, all bills to be introduced or amendments thereto moved in the State legislature and all orders, regulations, rules, by-laws issued by the state Government under the Constitution or any laws made by Parliament or the legislature of the State shall be published in the official Gazette in the Assamese language.

The Bengalis in Assam were not satisfied with the official Language Act. They formed the Nikhil Assam Bangabhasa Raksha Samiti and submitted a petition under Art. 347 to the President on 5th April 1961.

In Cachar, things moved in a different direction. The Congressmen adopted a militant attitude. They formed the Cachar Zilla Gana Sangrama Parishad which decided to launch a civil disobedience movement. The then Congress President Sanjeeva Reddi appealed to the Congressmen of Cachar not to participate in the Sangrama Parishad Movement, but they refused to listen to him. On 24 May 1961, a special convention of the DCC's decided to sever themselves from the APCC and directed the MLAs and the MPs to resign their membership of the legislature. The DCCs formed the Bhasha Andolan Samiti. The ACC which met at Duragapur decided to depute Lal Bahadur Shastri as peacemaker. After meeting all the parties to the dispute, Shastri formulated his proposals. First, the Assam official language Act be amended for the elimination of the provision relating to Mohkuma Parishads and Municipal Boards. Second, communications between the State Headquarters and Cachar and the Autonomous Hill districts should be in English until replaced by Hindi. Third, at the State level English should be used for the present. Later on, English would continue to exist along with Asaamese. Fourth, linguistic minorities in the State would be provided with safeguards suggested by the Government of India. Fifth, all Acts, Bills Ordinances, Regulations and orders would continue to be published in the official Gazette in English. Sixth, arrangements should be made for the effective implementation of development schemes at the district level. Finally, the agitation in Cachar should be withdrawn and those arrested in this connection should be released.

The legislature accepted the recommendations of Lal Bahadur Shastri. The language conflict came to an end for the present.

In 1970, the language again conflict broke out, as regards the medium of instruction. The matter was decided by the Supreme Court in favour of Assamese being the medium of instruction.

References

1. The Hindu, Madras.
2. Anandram Dekhial Phukan, The Case of Assamese

Language (1854) Nowgong.

3. Ibid. Anandram Phukan
4. letters to the Government, 1847.
5. Ibid.
6. Mills, A Report on Assam, 1854.
7. Ibid.
8. Letters to Government, Vol. 5, 1862.
9. Vol. 5, Letters to Government, 1862.
10. Assam Commissioner's office, File No. 471.
11. No. 1537 G. Education 19.5.1873, Bengal.
12. Officiating Inspector of Schools.
13. Two persons, Deonath Barua and Parmanand of Sibsagar petitioned to the Chief Commissioner, Home, July 1874.

5

The Autonomy Movements in Assam

Assam become a Chief Commissioner's province in 1874. Manipur, Tripura and Lushai Hills were not a part of the state at that time. Lushai Hills district was added by the end of the last century. Manipur was placed under the control of the Chief Commissioner of Assam. Soon after in 1905, Assam was merged with East Bengal. In 1912, the partition was annuled and there was no change in its area between 1912 and August 15, 1947.

There was always a demand for merger of Sylhet with Bengal sometimes by Hindus and at others by Muslims, and often the two communities and two Valleys worked at cross purposes. Mountbatton announced on 3 June 1947 that Sylhet would be merged with East Pakistan after a referendum. Accordingly, a referendum was held and Sylhet minus eight *thana* areas was merged with East Pakistan. Eight *thana* areas of Karimganj were merged with Cachar district. Bhutanese area of Eastern Dwars, annexed during the Bhutan war in 1866 remained part of Assam after 1874 and was transferred to Bhutan by the Assam Legislative Assembly and the Parliament.

The State Reorganisation Commission and the North-East

The North-East consisted of the following before the operation of the State Reorganisation Commission (S.R.C.):

(1) The State of Assam.

(2) The excluded area of North-East Frontier Agency (NEFA).

(3) Group C states of Manipur and Tripura, formerly princely states.

Different view-points were expressed about the re-organization of Assam before the S.R.C. Some of the demands were:

1. There was a demand for a Hill state comprising of all the hill districts included in part A of the Sixth Schedule, including Naga Hills.
2. The N. N. C. wanted separation from Assam and India.
3. The formation of Purbachal State consisting of the area around Cachar.
4. There was demand for the formation of Kamatapur State consisting of Goalpara, Garo Hills, Coach Bihar, Jalpaiguri and Darjeeling.
5. The Assam government along with Assam Pradesh Congress Committee, Tripura State Congress Committee and C.P.I. wanted *status quo*.
6. The government of Assam, however, was to welcome closer connection with NEFA and if possible the merger of Manipur, Tripura and Cooch Bihar.

The S.R.C. did not concede these demands. However, they wanted the merger of Tripura with Assam so as to have proper co-ordination in development work. They wanted Manipur to remain separate in order to maintain its individuality. Tripura was not merged with Assam and in effect the S.R.C. did not bring any change in North East India.

The Hill people of Assam, by and large did not accept the recommendations of the S.R.C. The Nagas continued to ask for autonomy and merger of contiguous Naga areas. The Naga Hills Tuensang Area, NHTA was formed in 1957 as a centrally administered area by the merger of the Naga Hills district of Assam and Tuensang Division of NEFA. It became the 16th State of Indian Union on December 1st 1963.

The formation of Nagaland had the following effects:

1. Manipur and Tripura felt ignored as they still remained Union territories and Nagaland became a state from a district. The process of formation of Manipur and Tripura states was hastened by the formation of Nagaland.
2. The possibility of statehood for smaller areas with a smaller population became the accepted morn.
3. The principle of linguistic states was successfully challenged and a new basis for statehood was found.
4. It generated hunger for political autonomy among the tribal communities of Assam, resulting in the demands for tribal states.
5. The insurgency in Nagaland sent wrong signals. The modus operandi of MNF and NNC has a lot of similarities.

The East India Tribal Union joined the Chaliha Ministry on the insistence of Pt. Nehru. They were mostly reconciled to their remaining in Assam. In the meantime, Assam Language Act, 1960, declaring Assamese as the state language was introduced. The tribal leaders protested and formed the All Party Hill Leaders Conference, APHLC was formed in 1960 to fight for a separate Hill state. Initially the Hill leaders did not aim at having hill state(s) . Capt. Sangma wanted greater autonomy for district councils. Perhaps it needed greater flexibility, tact and pragmatism at that juncture of history, which our leaders lacked.

Had they shown imaginativeness at the time, perhaps we may not have had to face the balkanization of Assam. The autonomy movements in North-East India took different routes in different states.

1. Arunachal Pradesh gradually emerged as a state through Union territory status. Its emergence as a state was a painless process. .

2. Meghalaya achieved statehood in a democratic process. As usual the repeated petitioning and agitations by A.P.H.L.C. leaders took place. The central government wanted to give greater autonomy to the Hill people through a number of plans such as the Scottish plan, the Nehru plan and the Mehta plan. The Pataskar Commission recommendations were tried in between. Ultimately, Meghalaya autonomous state was created. The name "sub-stated" was not acceptable. When the autonomous state experiment failed, the state of Meghalaya consisting of "united Khasi and Jayntia" and "Garo Hills" district was formed. The Mikir Hills (now Karbi Anglong) and North Cachar Hill districts were given the option to join Meghalaya, which they did not accept. Earlier they accepted the Mehta plan of autonomy.

3. The merger of the Mizo Union with APHLC did not last long. M.U. demanded a separate state for the Mizos. There was armed rebellion and insurgency in the Mizo Hills district following which the district was separated from Assam and made a Union territory. Ultimately it was made a state after the Mizo accord with Laldenga.

4. Manipur and Tripura which were initially princely states and then group C states, became union territories. Finally, they emerged as states along with Meghalaya.

5. Of late, Bodo inhabitated areas of the plains of Assam have got their regional council. The creation of seven states has not resulted in a conflict and tension free atmosphere in North-East India. The Karbis and Dimasa Cacharis and even Lalungs continue to ask for autonomy. The Hmars of Mizoram

continue to pose a problem for the Mizos and the country. The conflict between Bengalis and the tribals of Tripura and recent ethnic conflict between Nagas and Kukis of Manipur continue to worry conscious and conscientious citizens of the country.

I feel that there is need of constitutional change to ensure responsible functioning of autonomous political units of the country. The autonomous units should be made answerable for the failures of the planning process, resulting in perpetuation of poverty and suffering of the masses.

6

Genesis of the Autonomy Movement in Nagaland

Divided into as many as thirty two[1] known Naga Tribes with differences in traditions, customs, costumes, language, polity etc., the Nagas are people whose unity is found in diversity. They are a people with traditional pride and martial vigour, having abiding attachment to their clan and village for the preservation of which they are ever prepared to sacrifice their all. Though they lived in relative isolation in their inaccessible and rugged hilly terrains from days of yore they were accustomed to live in well organised village-republics which were like the ancient city-states of Greece, completely independent of one another. Small communities are always conducive to the growth of the spirit of patriotism and independence. The history of the Nagas is therefore, mainly the story of small but independent village-states. each fighting for its own supremacy over its neighbours.

Nagas Down the Ages

In the historical period, the Nagas for the first time came into contact with the Ahoms in the beginning of the 13th Century, but the Ahoms did not subjugate the Nagas and it was not part of their policy to bring them under their rule. The British who stepped into the shoes of the Ahoms in 1826, in the beginning did not follow any policy to annex their territories, but subsequently adopted a "forward policy" to suit their imperial interests which enabled them to establish mastery over a part of the Naga Hills. This position was, however, gained by the British, but not without a challenge from the valiant Nagas. In fact, the Nagas offered the stiffest possible resistance to the foreign invaders from the very beginning, but ultimately they had to concede defeat at the battle of Khonoma in 1879. So except from this time till the transfer of power by the British in August, 1947, the Nagas had never been part of what today constitutes the Indian nation. A hand-out, *Nagaland: A strange country in Asia*, published immediately after Independence, by Naga National Council aptly says :

In history, no enemy ever conquered the Nagas, except the British who conquered and occupied portions of Naga territory from 1879 to 1947, August 14th. The Nagas have not made any progress during the last seven decades. This is the truth and the source of all troubles.[2]

Effect of British Rule on the Nagas

Along with British rule came the introduction of western education, Christian religion and currency. While education and Christianity inculcated liberal ideas and national conciousness in the Naga mind, monetization helped the formation of a middle class in the hitherto casteless society of the Nagas. From the very beginning, the British tried to make the Nagas insular and the process was completed by the introduction of Inner Line Regulations in 1873 which prevented entry of people from the plains to the Naga Hills while making exceptions to European speculators and foreign missionaries.[3] Such a policy of segregation might have served be interests of the foreign rulers or to a limited extent of the Nagas, but the Nagas were cut off from the mainstream of Indian national life and they continued to live in tribal isolation which prevented them from taking part in the freedom struggle launched by the Indian National Congress.

In the matter of imparting education to the Nagas, the government adopted half-hearted measures allowing

Christian missionaries to undertake this task. It followed a policy of apathy and indifference in opening institutions of higher education to the Naga youths. The government was so allergic to the opening of High Schools that one of its high officials candidly said that English education would "spoil the Naga"[4]. In fact, by closing the door of higher education, the government wanted to keep them all of from the Swadeshi Movement which had assumed by then the character of a national upsurge all over the country. Notwithstanding such constraints on higher education, a few fortunate Naga youths who had the means, availed opportunities of higher education in places like Jorhat, Golaghat, Guwahati, Imphal, Calcutta etc. On completion of their education, several educated Nagas joined the public services in different capacities.

Impact of World War I and Simon Commission

When the First World War broke out in 1914, India contributed in men and money to the Empire. A considerable number of Nagas went to the European War Front. These men returned in the middle of 1918, not only with sufficient money, but with new ideas, standards and with the so-called impression of the "might of the *Sarkar*"[5]. The Nagas who had seen a new world came into contact with the advanced people of the West and became conscious that their interests and outlook should cross the bounds of their clan and village. In 1918, a few government officials and leading Naga Chiefs formed the "Naga Club" at Kohima for promoting the interest of the Nagas which for the first time provided a common forum for the leaders of different tribes of Nagas. When the Simon Commission visited Kohima in 1929, a strong delegation signed by as many as twenty members representing different Naga tribes submitted a memorandum to the Commission demanding that their hills should be excluded from the proposed reform scheme and kept under direct British rule to "save them from being overwhelmed by the people of the plains." "You are the only people who have even conquered us and when you go, we should be as we were", the delegation pointed out. The memorandum concluded with the demand that:

"If the British government, however, wants to throw us away, we pray that we should not be thrust to the mercy of people who could never have conquered us themselves and to whom we are never subjugated, but to leave us alone to determine for ourselves as in ancient times.[6]

According to Asuso Yonuo, the "asking for exclusion of Nagaland from the proposed reforms, however, precise in presentation, contained considerable political significance". "It emphatically pointed out", he continues "the obvious desire of the Nagas for the restoration of their independence which the British had snatched from them". In a rapidly changing situation, it was not at all surprising that the Nagas who were "never properly brought under Ahom rule or any other rule except the British", became very much concerned about their political emancipation.[7]

On the recommendation of the Simon Commission, the Government of India Act, 1935, excluded Naga Hills from the Reform Scheme and it was declared as an "Excluded Area" to be administered by the Governor of Assam according to his own discretion. Whether the special provisions made by the Act of 1935 have fulfilled the much desired political aspirations of the Nagas is difficult to say, but from the absence of any agitation of a political nature from the time of giving effect to the New Constitution (1 April, 1937) to the formation of Naga National Council (April, 1946) , it may be presumed that the Nagas more or less acquiesced in the new arrangement.

World War II and the Nagas

The Second World War (1939-45) had seen Nagaland as one of the theaters of the War: the Nagas were both physically and mentally affected by it. The Japanese invasion of Kohima led the British and their allies to mobilise men and supplies from India and abroad. While a section of the Nagas supported the Japanese masters, many supported the British. Despite acute hardship, devastation and uncertainities, the war had produced a ferment in the Naga mind. This was further aggravated by the Quit India Movement (1942), the invasion of Eastern India by the Azad Hind Fauz of Netaji Subhash Chandra Bose and subsequent political developments leading to the impending changes in the Indian political scene.

The most important outcome of the war as far as the Nagas were concerned was the emergence of a middle class in Nagaland.[8] The contact of this class with the people of different nations led to their wider outlook. Parochissm was now replaced by a growing sense of unity and Nagaism. They realised that the days of the British Raj were numbered and the idea of complete independence gripped the politically conscious Nagas who dreamt the dream of a nation of their own.

Naga National Council

The war had brought a greater degree of unity and cohesion among the different tribes of Nagas. After the war, at the initiative of C.R. Pawsey, the then Deputy Commissioner of the Naga Hill District in April, 1945, the Naga Hills District Council was formed on the nucleus of the erstwhile "Naga Club" for rehabilitation and reconstruction of war devastated areas of Nagaland. However, the fast changing political situation transformed it into the Naga National Council in the course of a year. The formation of the council was indeed a "major step in the consolidation of Naga nationalistic forces". The most significant fact about the council is that for the first time, the term "national" was used and the Naga National Council was composed of twnety nine members representing different tribes of Nagas on the basis of proportional representation.[9]

In this connection, it may be pointed out that in the late twenties of the present century when the idea of local self government was first contemplated in Naga hills, some such councils were organised on a tribe-wise basis. The roots of such a basis are to be found in the Christian Church organisations, such as the Angami Baptist Church, the Ao Bappist Church, the Lotha Baptist Church, the Sema Baptist Church etc. Frederick Downs rightly says that Christianity has played a significant role in bringing about unity of all Nagas, irrespective of their age-old traditions of inter-village and inter-tribal feuds and rivalries. He further adds that "In conventions and councils as well as in assemblies, different tribes were brought together which fostered a sense of tribal and regional identify for the first time" and "in truth provided foundations for modern conceptions of political identity though this was not a conscious objective of either the missions or the churches".[10]

Crown Colony Scheme

Being satisfied with the hill tribes' participation and help to the Government during the war, some top-ranking British officers suggested new plans for the administration of hill areas of North-East India. Since his retirement Sir Robert Neil Reid, a former Governor of Assam (1939-43) tried to rouse interest in this problem in England. Ever since the time of the Simon Commission, J.H. Hutton, Deputy Commissioner of Naga Hills District, J.P. Mills, Adviser to the Government of Tribal Affairs, made suggestions for the separation of hills from the plains and constituting these more or less into a "North-East province or agency".[11] Writing in the Geographical Journal entitled "*Excluded areas of Assam*" Reid said:

"We are responsible for the future welfare of a set of very loyal, primitive people who are habituated to look to us for protection, and who will get it from no other source. They are not by a hundred years ready to take their place in a democratic constitution or to compete with the sophisticated politician to place and power, and personally I have no doubt whatever to allow them in any way to be involved in Indian politics, and which, with no safeguards such as now exist, would spell disaster for them.

It is up to us to see that they are given, under our protection a period of respite, within which they will develop on their own lines and without outside interference."[12]

In this connection it may be pointed out that in "private and secret" correspondence dated 6 June 1944, to Mr. L.S. Amery, Secretary of State for India, Field Marshall Viscount Wavell while appreciating the Nagas against the Japanese during the war, wrote to Sir Andrew Clow, Governor of Assam as to what should be done to "reward the staunchness of these people, both immediately and later. It will probably be difficult to do very much for them, but I feel we must try". Andrew clow in his letter dated 19 April 1945 to Sir John Colville, Acting Governor General (21 March-4 June 1945) said:

"Accounts, generally somewhat imaginative, are circulating regarding the government's as yet unformulated intention in respect of the future of our frontier. In one such report which emanated, I believe, from Calcutta, Lord Wavell was credited with taking home a plan under which our hills and the adjoining hills of Burma and Bengal, could become a separate entity ruled solely by Great Britain. The tribal people themselves are beginning to take a more vocal interest in their own future. A recent conference in Shillong, while far from fully representative of the tribes, contained most of the more prominent men and inaugurated an "Assam Tribes and Races Federation". And a meeting of the Nagas at Kohima has asked to remain under the British Crown with their own Legislative Council."

The letter further stated :

"The most interesting feature of the Shillong is the combination of our plains and hill-tribals and their emphasis on their distinctness from India. Apparently assuming the success of the Pakistan campaign, they opposed emphatically their inclusion in either Pakistan or Hindustan. They also pressed for reforms and for the stoppage of immigration into Assam Valley. They appear to contemplate the retention of Assam proper as a unit, i.e. the exclusion of the Surma Valley which is properly a part of Bengal. The whole subject is a difficult one and is being examined in consultation with experts on External Affairs on the hills and indeed only on those hills which constitute our border. I hope to have discussions with *caroe* shortly, but until the constitutional future of India generally and Assam in particular is a good deal more clear than at present, any step likely to increase the separation of our hills from the plains would probably be unwise, and a division of our hill tribes into provincial and non-provincial is in my present judgment, something to be avoided.[12a]

Sharing similar views, but linking with the question of defence of the North East Frontier, Sir Reginald Coupland, a British Constitutional expert advocated a scheme of "Crown Colony" on a Civil Administrative Unit comprising the hill areas along the North East Frontier of Assam and taking in similar areas of Burma as well. According to him the inhabitants of both areas were alike in race and culture, and in no sense belonged to the Indian or Burmese nation.[13]

Impending Political Changes

In the meanwhile, with the coming to power of the Labour party in England led by Clement Attlee, events moved in rapid succession in Indian polities, resulting in the arrival of the Cabinet Mission proposals for resolving the political stalemate in India. Its proposals for an All India Federation, Grouping of provinces, formation of an Interim Government and a Constituent Assembly made it abundantly clear that Indian Independence was just around the corner. The freedom loving Nagas who were not involved in the national struggle were caught unawares and were in an utter state of confusion and uncertainty. Writing about the "Naga Search for Identity", a Naga intellectual said.

The fear of being placed under domination of a new Government of India and their dislike for the economically aggressive low-landers made the Nagas nervous about the prospect of their new relationship with the Government of India. This uneasiness also made them self-conscious about their distinctiveness from plainsmen and even led some of them to re-discover the elements of traditional culture which was common to all the Naga tribes.[14]

Naga National Council and Congress Leaders

In the beginning, the political objective of the Naga National Council was solidarity of all Nagas including those of the un-administered areas and the inclusion of their hills within the province of Assam in a free India with local autonomy and adequate safe-guards for the interests of the Nagas. This demand of the Nagas was well received in the circle of the Indian National Congress. Pandit Jawaharlal Nehru, the Congress president in his letter dated 5th August, 1946 to T. Sakhrie, Secretary of the Naga National Council while expressing satisfaction said :

"I am glad that the Naga National Council stands for the solidarity of all the Nagas tribes including those who live in the so-called unadministered territory. I agree entirely with your decision that the Naga Hills should constitutionally be included in an autonomous Assam in a free India with local autonomy and due safeguards for the interest of the Nagas."[15]

Phizo's Emergence in Naga Politics

Meanwhile on 2 September 1946, an Interim Government headed by Jawaharlal Nehru formally assumed office and a Constituent Assembly met on 9 December, to frame the constitution of the Union of India despite the opposition of the Muslim League. With the return of

Angami Zapu Phizo[16] from Burma and his entry into the political arena of Nagaland, an independent Nagaland outside the Indian Constitution became the rallying cry of a section of the members of the Naga National Council. It may be pointed out that Phizo during 1982 assisted the Japanese in Burma in the hope of getting Nagaland as an independent State after the war since then he must have developed his plan for an independent homeland for the Nagas in the event of British defeat.

Phizo through the Naga National Council sent a memorandum to the British Government on 20th February, 1947 for establishing an interim government for a period of ten years, at the end of which the Naga people could be left to choose any form of government under which to live. The Council in its memorandum openly stated that a constitution drawn up by people having no knowledge of the Naga Hills and its people will be quite "unsuitable and unacceptable" to the Nagas.[17]

Nine Point Agreement and Naga Delegation to Gandhi

In May, 1947 an Advisory Committee of the Indian Constituent Assembly headed by Gopinath Bordoloi came to Kohima and discussed with the Naga Leaders the points raised in the memorandum of 20 February, 1947. But the leaders insisted that the Bordalai Committee recommend to the Government to accept the points raised in the memorandum. The Committee expressed its inability to recommend the same as these would go outside the scope of the Constitution of India. After the failure of the Advisory Committee, Sir Akbar Hydari, Governor of Assam visited Kohima on 26th June, 1947 for a settlement with the Naga leaders. In this context, it may be stated that Sir Andrew Clow, the Predecessor of Hydari and Charles Pawsey (D.C. of Naga Hills) advised the Nagas to give up their demand for independence. Hydari after discussing with the Naga leaders and Pawsey for three days worked out a formula comprising nine points, for the solution of the Naga problem[18] Although on almost all the points except the last one, there was more or less agreement, the last point which read as follows proved controversial:

"The Governor of Assam as the agent of the Indian Union will have a special responsibility for a period of ten years to ensure the due observance of this agreement. At the end of this period the Naga National Council will be asked whether they require the above agreement to be extended for a further period or a new agreement regarding the future of the Naga people arrived at."

As regards this point, while the Naga National Council claimed that it ensured the Nagas right to complete independence at the end of the ten year period, the government side gave a different interpretation. Its stand was that the Nagas would be able to suggest changes in their administrative setup and receive greater autonomy within the Indian Union. As the stalemate continued, in order to resolve it, a delegation of Naga National Council headed by Phizo met Mahatma Gandhi at the Bhangi Colony in New Delhi.[19] Phizo conveyed to Gandhi the Naga's determination to stay out of the Indian Union. Gandhi told the Naga delegation thus :

"Nagas have every right to be independent. We did not want to live under domination of the British and they are now leaving us. I want you to feel that India is yours. I feel that the Naga Hills are mine, the matter must stop there. I believe in the brotherhood of man, but I do not believe in force or forced union. If you do not wish to join the Union of India, nobody will force you to do that."[20]

Hardening of Naga Attitude

In fact, they received from Gandhi nothing but his exhortation to become good citizens and to learn the real significance of the word "independence". Failing to get any assurance of support in their cause, on their return to the hills they declared on the August 14, the independence of Nagaland, i.e. a day earlier to the declaration of independence by India. This declaration by itself opened a new chapter in the history of Nagaland. It ushered in an area of confrontation and conflict, offensive launched by the Indian Security Forces against the Nagas and counter offensive by the latter. The assumption of direct leadership of the Naga National Council by Phizo in 1949[21], referendum of May 1951, boycott of general elections in 1952, creation of Naga Hills Tuensang Area under Ministry of External Affairs in 1957, attainment of statehood by Nagaland in December, 1963, Peace Mission and the Cease Fire Agreement of 1964, Shillong Accord of November 1975, meeting between the then Indian Prime Minister Morarji Desai and Phizo in London 1978 are important political developments which require no elaboration.

Confrontation between NNC and Government of India and Peace Missions

To come back to the question of Nagas demand for autonomy, one must admit that the British during their actual rule of seven decades kept the freedom-loving Nagas isolated from the rest of the sub-continent. They were thus kept aloof from the freedom struggle led by the Indian National Congress. Suddenly they were forced to join the Indian Union without their consent on the eve of British departure by the India Independence Act (1947). No genuine attempt was made to appreciate the demand of the Nagas and their standpoint. From the beginning, the Indian leaders did not try to win the Naga people or convince them of the impracticability of their existence as an independent state outside India. The last article of the Hydari Agreement ought not to have been kept vague or ambiguous. As Phizo was in virtual control of the Naga National Council and as the unquestioned leader of the Nagas, the Indian leaders ought to have given him time for a negotiated settlement of the issue, but instead of doing so the crackdown on the members of the Naga National Council was an unwise step as it only hardened the demand of the Nagas. The formation of the state of Nagaland in 1963 simply divided the Nagas into two camps. The most fundamental mistake on the part of the Assam and Central Governments was to treat the problem as one of purely law and order, they from the beginning minimised the intensity of the genuineness of Nagas search for identity. Even the Peace Mission belatedly appreciated the genuine desire of the Nagas for self determination and their struggle for the preservation of their way of life. Jayprakash Narayan, a member of the Peace Mission openly declared :

"There can be no doubt that the struggle led by the MFG cannot be regarded as a mere problem of law and order. It is most certainly a struggle for national freedom. It does not aim at over throwing a government, but it certainly aims at throwing out a government, namely, the Government of India, which it regards as established here by force. the Naga people are unquestionably a nation. While there can be no doubt that the Naga problem is not a law and order question, but a question of freedom for the Nagas, I have also tried to show that the Naga Freedom Movement may take a different character if it is placed in the context of a union of self-governing states.[22]"

Notwithstanding the failure of the Peace Mission to bring about a solution of the vexed Naga problem, the Peace Mission openly acknowledged the fact that the Nagas constitute a separate nation and that any Union of the Nagas with India had to be with the consent of the Nagas.[23] Today the Naga's assertion of a separate identity, political and cultural, are genuine. Though various factors are involved in bringing about the consciousness of ethnic identity, Christianity has been playing an important part in uniting the Nagas, irrespective of their age-old inter-tribal and inter-village feuds. Religion has been acting as a centripetal force in uniting the different Naga tribes of Nagaland, Manipur, Arunachal Pradesh etc. under a common identity "Naga".[24]

In recent years, Christianity has been blamed for arousing the new political consciousness of the Nagas inhabiting the North Eastern region. The missionaries have been made the "scape goat" for the political unrest in Nagaland. The Naga demand for independence or self determination which has been often associated with the activities of foreign missionaries should be understood in its historical context. It is true that by sheer devotion and dedication, the foreign missionaries endeared themselves to the Naga masses. While these missionaries penetrated into the interiors of their hills and some of them spent the best part of their lives amongst them, very little attempt was made by people of the plains to settle down in the hills and work for them. Apart from the lack of initiative on the part of plainsmen, their entry into the Naga Hills was restricted by the then Government. This had definitely enabled the foreign missionary to build up a favourable image for himself and a strong hold in the Naga mind. Taking advantage of it, individual missionaries who could not reconcile themselves to the political changes in the country after 15 August, 1947 might have dreamt the dream of a "Christian State" in the north-eastern region. This might have provided a source of encouragement for the Naga demand for separation from India from whose mainstream, they had already been kept aloof by the British policy of exclusion. Such activities of a political nature of individual missionaries should not be construed to mean that either the church or Christianity was at fault.[25]

There is no evidence in records to prove the Christian Church's involvement in the Naga demand for independence.

Writing about the search for new identity among the tribals of Manipur, T. S. Gangte says that this new awareness of the different groups of Nagas being one people under the Naga identity is indeed a "spectacular phenomenon". He further adds that the term "Naga" has become a "prestigious ethnic identity" and the emergence of Nagas in the political limelight of the whole North-East region during the fifties and sixties was due to the charismatic personality of Phizo.

The same scholar further says that a Naga, whether he is Angami, Ao, Kabui, Konyak, Lotha or Tangkhul prefers to call himself a "Naga" despite his separate tribal identity.[26]

A very proper assessment of the Naga autonomy movement has been made by another Naga scholar professor Gangmumei Kabui in the following words :

"Naga Independence Movement is a multi-faceted phenomenon. It is a search and assertion of the ethnic identity of the Nagas, articulated by the Naga elite represented by the charismatic personality of Phizo. It is a process of absorption of various tribes into a common nationality, motivated by a common political goal. It is also a product of the British colonial rule which enforced a common generic name "Naga" for the different tribes brought under a single administrative roof and law, accompanied by introduction of English education and Christianity spread by the supporters of the colonial rule.[27]"

Phizo's Meeting with Morarji Desai

Phizo had been staying in London since 1957. In June 1978, during the visit of the then Indian Prime Minister Morarji Desai, there was a meeting between him and Phizo. But as Phizo insisted on Naga independence, his meeting with the Indian Prime Minister bore no fruit. Such meetings were not followed by the successive Prime Minister Indira Gandhi and Rajiv Gandhi.

Hence, there was no further approach for a solution of the Naga problem at a higher level. Although the political situation in Nagaland considerably changed since the signing of the Cease Fire Agreement and Shillong Accord, peace was very often broken by both the parties, When a special Representative of the Assam Tribune met Phizo in London in July, 1978 and questioned him about the political situation in Nagaland, he told the former that the situation in Nagaland was not peaceful as asserted by the State and Central Governments. Again when the particular representative pointed out to him that there was peace in Nagaland and the political problem was solved, Phizo replied that whenever a territory was under army occupation there was peace of the grave and elections held under such a situation was never the correct indication of the mood of the people.[28]

Phizo who wanted to have a second round of talks with the Indian prime Minister for a political settlement of the Naga problem did not get any chance due to the fall of Morarji's Government. His successors Indira Gandhi and Rajiv Gandhi also did not take up the Naga issue with Phizo. Although Phizo is now no more in the world of the living, his supporters, the underground Nagas have not given up their hope for a settlement of the Naga problem of an autonomous Nagaland on which depends the well being of the Nagas. It would be a mistake to think that the Naga problem has vanished into thin air with the passing a way of that legendary figure. To conclude in the words of the first Chief Minister of Nagaland.

It (Naga problem) is a forest fire, sometimes it burns the foliage in the ground and sometime the flames reach the tree tops. But the fire remains in some form or other.

Notes and References

1. Horam, M., Naga Polity, page-27.
2. Naga National Council, Nagaland : A strange Country in Asia. page-4.
3. Chaube, S. K., Hill Politics in North East India. Page-14.
4. Report on the Progress of Education in E. B. and Assam (1901-2-1906-7) pages-108-9.
5. Reid, R. N., History of Frontier Areas Bordering on Assam, page-163.

6. Yunuo, A: The Rising Nagas, pages-132-3.
7. Ibid.
8. Chaube, S. K. ; OP Cit. page-40.
9. Misra, U. ; "The Naga National Question, " Reprint from Economic and Political weekly, Vol-XIII No.: 14 8th April, 1978. pages 618-22.
10. Downs, F. S., Christianity in N. E. India. page-165.
11. Chaube, S. K., OP Cit. page 69. Yonue, A.; Op Cit. page-140.
12. (a) Constitutional Relation Between Britain and India: The Transfer of Power (1942-7) , Vol. IV Nos 527, pages 1002-8 and Vol V No. 167 pages-9123.
13. Yunuo, A. ; OP Cit. page-140.
14. Moases and, P. ; "Naga Search for Identity" in National Seminar on Hill People in N.E. India, Calcutta, Dec. 1966. page-12.
15. Quoted in Ghosh, B.B.; History of Nagaland, page-1 59-60.
16. Angami Zapu Phizo who died in London, was born in 1904 in the village of Khonoma. He started his career as a businessman, and served in the I. N. A. of Subhash Bose from 1943-45. He was imprisoned in Rangoon Jail by the British and after his release returned to Naga Hills and joined the Naga National Council and became its president in 1950. At the request of the Naga people Phizo remained in London since 1857 till his death. Phizo's wide ranging contact, patriotism, foresight and the emergence of a number of independent communities in S. E. Asia caught his imagination and provided inspiration for the demand of a sovereign and independent Nagaland.
17. Yunuo, A., OP Cit. page-167.

18. Ibid. pages-171-8.
19. Ibid.
20. Ibid.
21 Ibid.
Yunuo, A., Op Cit. pages-181-2.
22. Bhattacharjee, A., Political Evolution of Nagaland. page-82.
23. Misra, U. ; Op Cit. page-621.
24. Downs, F. S. ; Op Cit. page 165.
25. Barpujari, S. K.; Early Christian Mission in the Naga Hills, Journal of Indian History, vol. XLVII, August 1970, pages 434-5.
26. Cangte, T.S. ; Search for New Identity, Man and Life, Vol-X, Nos. 3-4, July-Dec. 1984, page-180ff.
27. Kabui, G.; Ethnicity and State Formation, in N. E. India Journal, Department of History, Manipur University, Vol. II 1987.
28. Interview of Naresh Rajkhowa, Special Representative of the Assam Tribune in London with A. Z. Phizo in London. See the Assam Tribune 9th July, 1978.

7

Autonomy Movements in the Naga Hills District

The term 'autonomy' employed by the very early writers is distinctly political, signifying civil or national independence. Some authors of the 17th and 18th century used it to denote the freedom of the religious conscience. Kant introduced it in the language of moral philosophy. By "autonomy of the will" Kant means the faculty that the will possesses of being its own law giver, of being itself, by its own nature the source and substance of the moral law, or the moral law itself. But the will is autonomous only when it acts according to the moral law. Now the term autonomy is employed to all aspects of human life.

The autonomy movement in the Naga Hill district is of recent origin. Before tracing the autonomy movement in the district, it is essential that we have an understanding of the constitutional position of the Naga Hills District before Independence.

Constitutional position

Before the introduction of the Reforms of 1919, the whole of Assam, as constituted in 1874 was declared to be a scheduled district under the Scheduled District Act of 1974.

The justification for treating Assam, as a Scheduled District must be sought in the fact that a very large portion of the area was covered with hills, and peopled by primitive tribes. Further, the area population and revenue were also small. The area was full of tensions: religious, social, economic, regional and linguistic, between the two valleys which were the most advanced regions of the province. Sir B.N. Rao, the Legal Remembrancer of the Government of Assam, went to the extent of suggesting that since the conditions and interests of the two valley were fundamentally different, there should be separate administrations in both the valleys if real advance towards responsible government was to be made.

In 1917, the Montagu-Chelmsford report recommended that typically backward tracts should be excluded from the jurisdiction of the Reformed Councils. The implication of this recommendation is that if a territory is wholly excluded from the Reformed Scheme, no resolution should be enacted and no resolution should be moved in the Legislative Council affecting the area concerned. Legislation for such areas should be undertaken entirely by the means of Regulations made by the Governor-General in Council under the Government of India Act, 1915.

The recommendations of the Joint Report were referred to two experienced officers for their comments. Reid and Barnes were strongly in favour of the recommendation of the Report. They thought that the Naga Hills District should not be brought under the Reformed Council. A similar view was expressed by the Chief Commissioner. The Functions Committee, popularly known as the Southborough Committee supported the recommendation of the Joint Report. But the Southborough Committee also recommended that the Excluded Areas should be taken over by the Government of India and administered by them.

The Government of India, while accepting the first part of the recommendation of the Southborough Committee namely that the typically backward tracts should not be brought under the Reformed Council, did not agree with the second part, namely that the administration of the Excluded Areas should be the concern of the government. They pointed out a number of difficulties in the way of accepting the second recommendation. We need not go into the details of this.

The Government of India recommended that the backward tribes should be categorised into, excluded areas and the areas in which the Reforms Scheme could be introduced. The Naga Hills were completely excluded and therefore the Reforms Scheme was not introduced.

The Government of India Bill containing the recommendations of the Government of India was referred to the Joint Select Committee of the views expressed by the witnesses were considered by the Select Committee which also made its own recommendations that were embodied in the Government of India Act 1919. The Government of India Act, 1919, held, that the Governor General in Council, shall declare any territory in British India to be a backward area under the Government of India Act. On 3 January, 1920, the Governor General in Council declared the Naga Hills as a backward tract. It was also declared that all laws passed by the Provincial and Central legislatures solely intended for those tracts shall apply, with previous consent of the Governor.

The Instrument of Instructions enjoined the Governor to promote the welfare of the tracts committed to his charge. For the implementation of this instruction, the Governor laid down that all proposals which would affect the backward tracts and all postings to the backward tracts should be submitted to the Governor. His decision in these matters was final and the government should implement it. Thus, the Ministers had no control over the administration of the Naga Hills district.

In 1927, some of the members of the Simon Commission visited Kohima to discuss the reforms to be introduced in the Naga Hills. The Naga Club said that they were not in need of any reforms. The Naga Club in a memorandum submitted to the Simon Commission demanded the exclusion of the Naga Hills District. It said, "We the undersigned Nagas of the Naga Club, who are the only persons who can voice the needs of our people, have heard with great regret that our Naga Hills are included within the reformed scheme of India without our knowledge. But as the administration of our Hills continued to be in the hands of the British officers, we did not consider it necessary to raise any protest in the past. Now we learn that you have come to India as the representatives of the British Government to enquire into the working system of government and the growth of education, and we beg to submit below our view with the prayer that our Hills may be withdrawn from the referred scheme and placed outside the Reforms but directly under the British Government. We never ask for any Reforms and we do not wish for any Reforms."

The inclusion of the Naga Hills District in the reformed constitution was opposed by officials and non officials. The most notable opponent of inclusion of Naga Hills District was the eminent social anthropologist, Dr. J. H. Hutton. Hutton spent long years in the Naga Hills District as its Deputy Commissioner and made a thorough study of the Naga problem. In a special note prepared for the Government of Assam, Hutton said categorically that the interests of the Hill Districts would not be served best by their inclusion in the constitutional Reforms. On the other hand they would suffer by being joined with the people of an irreconcilable culture in an unnatural union which would ultimately harm both the parties. Hutton gave reasons in support of his opinion. This document is too long even in summary, to quote here.

The Government of Assam generally accepted the opinion of Hutton and recommended to the Simon Commission in 1928, the exclusion of the Naga Hills District from the Province of Assam, their administration being entrusted to the Government in Council and financed by the Central Government. The Government of Assam said,

"There is no sympathy on either side and the Union is an unnatural and artificial one resented by both the parties".

In 1930, the question of inclusion or exclusion of the Hill areas was again discussed by the Government of Assam. The Government of Assam recommended the exclusion of the Naga Hills District from the Reformed Council.

The Government of Assam also suggested the formation of the North Eastern Frontier Province consisting of all the hill areas including the Naga Hills district.

The Simon Commission generally accepted the recommendation of the Government of Assam. But the Commission made certain changes in the recommendation of the Government of Assam. It classified the backward tracts into two excluded and partially excluded areas. The excluded areas were somewhat advanced, though not competent to take full share in the reformed constitution. But the Simon Commission did not classify the tribal areas into two, this task being left to the government.

The recommendation of the Simon Commission was referred to Dr. Hutton. Dr. Hutton adhered to his original opinion and recommended the exclusion of the Naga Hills District from the reformed constitution.

The Government of India Bill 1935, included the recommendation of the Simon Commission. The Bill was referred to the Joint Select Committee which embodied the recommendation in the Sixth Schedule to the Act. When the Bill was introduced in the Commons, there was animated discussion. The Secretary of State withdrew the Sixth Schedule and promised to make a fresh enquiry into the matter and the final decision would be issued in the form of Order in Council. The Order in Council generally accepted the recommendation of the Simon Commission and the Naga Hills District was classified as an excluded area. Thus, the Naga Hills district was not under the Assam Legislative Assembly till 1947, when India became independent.

After Independence

When India was at the threshold of independence, there was a discussion about the future of the Naga Hills District. In the district, there was a well-organised political party, the Naga National Council. The N.N.C. met on 19th June, 1945 and drafted a memorandum for submission to His Majesty's Government. It was approved by the General Body of the N.N.C. which met at Wokha. It dealt with the future of the Naga Hills District. Clause 1 read as follows:

The Naga National Council stands for the solidarity of all Naga tribes including those of the unadministered areas. Then, the N.N.C. resolved, "The Council strongly protests against the grouping of Assam with Bengal."

The Council resolved, "The Naga Hills should be constitutionally included in an autonomous Assam in a Free India with local autonomy, and the interests of the Nagas duly safe guarded."

Finally, the N.N.C. resolved, "The Naga tribes should have a separate electorate." From the above, it is crystal clear that the N.N.C. agreed to be in India and that the Naga Hills district should form a part of the province of Assam. This attitude was maintained by the N.N.C. till November 1946, with the exception of the Konoma group comprising the villages with a population of 5000, who were talking of independence.

The N.N.C. changed its mind in February 1947. On 10 February 1947, the N.N.C. drafted a memorandum of self-determination for submission to H.M. Government and the Government of India. The N.N.C. met in Kohima and resolved to demand self determination for the Nagas. This meant that an interim government should be set up for a period of ten years at the end of which the Naga people would be free to choose any form of Government under which they would live.

The Nagas argued that:

a. Ethnically the Nagas constitute a distinct people.

b. The Nagas have a distinct social life, manner of living, laws and customs. Even their method of government of the people is quite different.

c. In religion, a great majority of the Nagas were animists, though Christianity was becoming more popular.

Such factors as the above make it imperative that the Nagas must have a separate form of government.

The N.N.C. argued that the Nagas have had no connection with the politics and policies of the different groups of the Indian politician. "Ought the British Government or the Government of Indian throw this society into the heterogenous mixture of the Indian races? Thrown among the crores of the Indian people, the one million Nagas with their unique system of life will be wiped out of existence. Hence this earnest plea of the Nagas for a separate form of Interim Government to enable them to grow to a full stature, with financial provision for a period of ten years at the end of which the Naga people will be left to select any form of government under which they themselves choose to live.

Now a question arises as to why the N.N.C. changed its position and demanded self determination. In 1945 the Nagas agreed to be a part of India, but in 1947, they demanded self determination. The Naga delegation that appeared before the Bordoloi Committee gave some reasons but they are not very convincing. They admitted that there were other factors but the exact nature of the factors was not stated. I think that it was Kevichusa who gave the reasons for the change of their attitude. Kevichusa said:

"When we passed the resolution (at Wodha) we were thinking of autonomous Assam and of free India, I mean a united India. But developments in India have taken a different shape and we cannot wait... So we have taken a decision on different lines. That is the reason for the change. "There may be other reasons", admitted the witness. But those reasons were not stated. I presume, I may be wrong, I beg to be excused that the Konoma group of villages which were talking of independence when the Wokha resolution was passed, must have seized the N. N.C. and driven out the moderates.

What is an interim government? Kevichusa explained it as a "Government of the Naga people by the Naga people" and that the people would run their own show with little or no disturbance from the outside and during the period of that ten years they would be able to make a responsible choice.

Later on, the N.N.C. said that they would have guardian power. This was not mentioned in the memorandum submitted to the H. M. Government. What is this guardian power? Anyone would give the N.N.C. financial aid during the period of ten years. This guardian power might be the H.M.G., or the Government of India or the Government of Assam.

What were the powers and functions of the guardian power? Its powers and functions were severely limited. First, it should maintain a force for the defence of the Naga Hill district and the Interim Government. The force maintained by the guardian power at its own expense should be responsible to the N.N.C. and the N.N.C. would be responsible to the guardian power. Second, the guardian power must give sufficient money for the maintenance of the interim government which would be in the hands of the N.N.C. without attaching any strings. The amount of financial aid shall be determined by mutual discussion between the parties concerned. The N.N.C. may submit its budget to the guardian power and indicate the defect in it. The guardian power was at liberty to determine the financial aid without attaching any conditions. The guardian power was thus connected with the N.N.C. only with regard to defence and financial aid.

It would not interfere in the internal administration of the Interim Government. The N.N.C. would have complete freedom to manage or mismanage its affairs. Further the strength of the defence force to be maintained by the guardian power would be determined by the N.N.C. after discussion with the guardian power. Thus, the guardian power would only have limited powers.

Again, the Interim Government would have full powers to raise revenues and its expenditure but the guardian power would finance the deficit. It may discuss the amount of grant in aid that must be given but it could not attach any conditions to it.

On 19th May 1947, the Dimapur Tribal Union Society resolved:

(1) That the Tribal People (of the Naga Hills) desire that they and their territories remain included in Assam as their ethnological, geographical historical and cultural affinity demand that they keep so united.

(2) That the tribal people (of the Naga Hills) desire to be a part and parcel of Assam.

(3) The tribal council demands the protection of their minority rights, and joint electorate with reservation of seats.

(4) That the classification of the tribal areas into excluded and partially excluded should be abolished and all the tribal areas should be included and placed under the administrative control of Assam.

(5) The tribal council supported the views expressed by Sir Andrew Clow, the Governor of Assam.

Replying to an address at Mokokchung in the Naga Hills, presented by the Sub Divisional Committee, Sir Andrew dealt with the constitutional future of the Hills of Assam. He said that the British Government was withdrawing and the future Government of India, including

Assam and the Hills was a matter for the people of the land to decide. The Constituent Assembly which was charged with the duty of working out plans for the future had already started work in Delhi and it would have to consider in due course the position of the Hill People.

A few of the Nagas had spoken of setting themselves up as a separate nation. But in his opinion it was not practicable for any section of Naga people or even all them to form a separate state or even a separate province. If they did that they would always remain poor and backward, their needs in respect of education, communication and health could not be met and they would lose even the inadequate services they were now enjoying. His advice therefore was that they should aim at reaching an accomodation with the people of the plains of Assam, which would be of mutual benefit to both. Their differences from the people of the plains were many and the leaders of the plains of Assam recognised them all and it should not be difficult to ensure that all that was best in their way of life, in their culture, and in their customs, would be preserved within the sphere of the local authority which they might expect to enjoy. They should remember that there are other Hill people who are facing the same difficulties, with whom they should cooperate.

The people of the Naga Hills should think not only of what they could secure, but also of what they could give. The Hill people of Assam have had a long experience in pure democracy, They understand that democracy does not mean, as some suppose, the rule of the majority, but the rule of the people as a whole and the Naga people can contribute positively to the maintenance of democracy in India. They can have a share in the government of their own hills, and as education develops, in the government of the province and he hoped that the Naga people ultimately would make a valuable contribution to the government as a whole.

Sir Andrew Clow was succeeded by Sir Akbar Hydari, who persuaded the Nagas to see reason and tread the path of practical politics. He succeeded in concluding the Nine Point Agreement which, however, died a natural death before the ink with which it was written dried up.

The political developments that have taken place in the Naga Hill Districts are so well known that they need no repetition.

path of practical politics. He succeeded in concluding the Nine Point Agreement which, however, died a natural death before the ink with which it was written dried up.

The political developments that have taken place in the Naga Hill Districts are so well known that they need no repetition.

8

Social Change and Conflict In Tribal Society

Modernisation and change are new phenomena in the tribal areas of North-East India. Modern education, monetary-economy, urbanization and greater exposures have developed in the process.

In many areas such as Nagaland, Meghalaya, Mizoram, and hills of Manipur, Christianity has taken the place of animism and has acted as a powerful agent of social change.

Social change is however, not a painless process. It has created a conflict situation between the traditional and new elites in the Society.

In this paper, I have used data of Nagaland and that of Chang Nagas for illustration. The findings have wide application.

The Chang Nagas inhabiting Tuensang districts of Nagaland were grouped among the Central Nagas by J.H. Hutton. They do not have their written history. There is no mention of them in the old Assam diary of the Deputy Commissioner of Naga Hills in the later half of the last century. Their history may be divided into the following phases:

The early History and the Chang identity formation

Although they do not have a written history, their

legends help us in understanding the process of ethnic mix and fusion responsible for Chang identity formation. While the Changpang legend links them with Kenyaks and Phens, the Langa legend points towards their link with Yingchungris, Kenyakas, Sangtams and Phems. Similarly some believe in the Ao legend of Longsterek, which confirms the mixed origin of the Chang tribe. This confirmation is further strengthened by the fact that the Chang language has four dialects which are akin to different tribal dialects, and that they have corresponding clans with that of other Naga tribes, specially the Aos. This period of Chang identity formation was complete by 1880 A.D.

Emergence of British rule in the Chang neighbourhood

The second period in the Chang Naga History started around 1880 A.D. and continued upto the First World War. This was the period of greater exposure of the change with the outside world leading to compromise with the new social realities. The punitive expeditions led by the British against their head hunting raids made them realise that they would have to leave their old habits of head hunting sooner or later. This period also saw the emergence of Debhashis as a powerful group, with administrative and judicial powers leading to the gradual decrease of the powers of the village authorities. Many Changs went to schools and became Christians during this period.

Phase of greater identity formation

This phase of Chang history started during the First World War and lasted upto the formation of Nagaland State on December 1, 1963. For the first time, a group of Chang Nagas had the chance of being together with other Nagas as members of Naga Labour Corps during the First World War in France. They developed a sense of belonging towards each other and thus the process of Naga identity formation started. Many Changs earned huge incomes and thus were exposed to the momentary economy,

Formation of Naga National Council and its branches in the Chang area, Chang Naga participation in the underground movement under the leadership of Thungdi Chang and their participation in the three Naga People's conventions led to the strengthening of this new identity. The Chang area merged with another Eastern Naga area when administration was started to form Tuensang district after independence. In 1957 Tuensang district was merged with Naga Hills district to form Nagaland Tuensang area (NHTA), a centrally administered territory. The administrative and constitutional evolution was complete in December 1963 with the emergence of Nagaland as the Sixteenth state of Indian Union.

Phase of Development and Rapid Social Change

The establishment of schools, construction of new roads, business centres etc, followed the establishment of administrative centres. However, all such development activities started with greater pace only after the statehood.

The Changs continued to observe various rituals and ceremonies during different phases of their life from birth to death. With the change of religion and advent of administration, many rituals, ceremonies, social institutions and usages have either radically changed or been abandoned. The Changs no more join their morungs (Haki) nor do they sleep in their respective youth dormitories (Sechem and Shemshimang). The Baptist Christians consider Haki as a heathen institution. As a result, many Hakis were burnt down or left to rot and on their place imposing church buildings were constructed. Resounding drums have been silenced and head hunting and related war - dances and songs have become matter of the past.

A remarkable change has occurred in the case of names. Previously individuals used only their personal names and no surname. Today, they use the name of their tribe and clan as their surname. A new trend is either to prefix or suffix the name of the father with the personal name. The personal names in the past often denoted prowess in war or generosity in feasts and such names were often inherited by a person from his ancestors and others were debarred from using them. No such bar exists nowadays in their society. There is also a tendency to use either a biblical name or a name related to or derived from a biblical theme.

The student community and the Christian missionaries opposed tattooing. As a result such practices are no longer common. They also opposed burial inside the house and therefore, we find graves outside the village. Some of the customs related to child birth, naming, marriage etc. which do not have religious overtones continues to exist.

The social structure of the Chang society favoured assimilation of diverse ethnic elements. Such assimilation was done by conquest, adoption and marriage. They followed two kinds of adoption - Sholalibti and Bumbti. In the former one, the adopted person completely submerged his or her identity in the adopter's family without any future social disability. In the latter case, the adopted person maintained a separate identity, while the process was reversible and the adopter had certain social disabilition. This process of adoption worked well in their society and even persons coming from far away places and speaking different languages used to completely forget their different ethnic origins and become Changs in a few generations. A recent example of such adoption is the Puthambeu Village, a village of Nepali settlers, who have become Chang by this process. Similarly, the majority population of Noka and Lengla was Ao a few generations ago.

Family continues to be the basic unit of Chang society. The increasing individualism has not affected it adversely and in fact it has strengthened it. On the other hand, the clan and village solidarity is weakening day by day. Previously it was essential for every village to have settlers from each clan in it. Nowadays it is not necessary. The prohibition of marriage in the corresponding clan of other tribes still continued to have force. Thus, the clan continues to regulate marriage.

The economic life of the Chang Nagas continues to be centred round shifting cultivation as the means of their livelihood. Fishing, hunting and food gathering are still practiced. All these activities have been adversely affected due to the changing patterns of labour. The decay in the age old practice of organisation of labour based on age groups is taking place due to following reasons:

i) Young ones are attending their schools and are not equipped for manual work.

ii) The old social values of mutual help and cooperation have lost their mooring and clan and kinship ties have weakened under the heavy sway of individualism. The social structure has lost its cohesiveness and resilience.

iii) The cash economy has affected social behaviour as the villagers now work for others on daily wages basis. Inspite of such a change, however, egalitarian feelings still persist and no wage-earner is treated as servant or labourer.

The distribution of land holding in the Chang villages is not even and as a result, share croping is practiced in most of the villages. The surplus of food-grains produced by the rich farmers is either marketed in the nearby towns or kept as buffer stock against possible crop failure. Some foodgrain is also either given as loan or distributed to needy persons. Feasts of merits rarely have an attraction for the Chang Nagas nowadays due to the following reasons:

a) The Christians associate it with old heathen, religion and practices.

b) The growing trend of individualism hinders individuals from any such social expenditure. Thus feasts of merit for which every rich farmer used to have special charms as it used to bring ceremonial prestige to the feast giver have lost their charm and the farmer has lost an extra incentive for surplus crop production.

The advent of modern administration and monetary economy have resulted in the diversification of the traditional economy and opening of up new sources of income. The administration headquarters provide a readymade market for the sale of grains, vegetables, fruits, meat, fish, milk, forest product and fuelwood. There was a change in the agricultural production pattern in the villages and they started producing more and more cash crops such as vegetables, chillies, ginger, fruits etc. The people also started raising cattle, pigs, hen as well as pisci culture.

Thus the market economy necessitated diversification of production in their area. It also considerably helped occupational mobility and more and more persons wanted to earn money by various ways such as, government service, daily wage earning, contract and supply, trade and commerce, money lending etc.

Most of the traders in tribal areas are non tribal. This creates socio-psychological communication barriers between the tribal people and others. Underdeveloped road network creates physical communication barriers and thus imperfect markets exist.

The markets have exposed people to new items of consumption, which may only be procured with cash. This has upset the age old customary system of barter exchange based on face to face relationship between the co-villagers. Thus a very rapid change is taking place in the simple and undifferentiated structure of tribal economy under the new pressures generated by market economy.

The shops in remote areas such as in Tuensang and

other towns are full of good clothes, shoes, utensils, radios, tape recorders, cosmetics, furniture etc. for which every villager shows interest. However, these items may only be purchased with cash. Thus the market creates the need of money, and act against barter trade.

As the markets create the need for money, many people who could not earn it were subjected to indedebtedness. The interests charged on money as well as grain loan is usually very high. Many persons sell their lands to repay the debt.

The government aimed at improving the lot of the rural people by implementing various schemes through its development departments and agencies. The main thrust of the government was in the field of agriculture and animal husbandry. The government granted subsidies and loans for converting their *Jhum* land into terraced fields. However, progress in this field was not satisfactory. Indiscriminate cutting of forests on the hill tops resulted in drying of water sources. Thus many newly constructed terraced fields were abandoned. Haphazard sanctioning of irrigation channels to individuals without proper planning resulted in misuse of scarce and precious water resources as well as internal strife between the villagers. The use of high yielding hybrid seeds, fertilizers and insecticides could not become popular. Same was the case with double cropping.

The different poverty alleviation programmes namely, IRDP (Integrated Rural Development Programme), TRYSEM (Training Rural Youth for Self Employment), NREP (National Rural Employment Programme) are run by the Rural Development Department in Nagaland. The establishment of the Village Development Board (VDB) as the kingpin of rural development is a new and welcome phenomenon. Its functioning as a village level voluntary body is by and large successful. The confidence of the villagers in this body is gradually increasing with the growing awareness among them about its aims and objectives.

Like the Village Development Boards (VDB), Village Common Fund is also an innovative idea in Nagaland. The Village Development Boards raise voluntary contributions from the villagers and deposit them in the bank for five years as fixed deposit. Government pays equal matching grant upto maximum of Rs. 75,000/- to each VDB so that the deposit becomes double. In Nagaland records are not available and therefore banks find it difficult to advance loan for any enterprise. Now such loans are advanced by the banks to villagers through the VDB for any enterprise against the security provided by the common fund deposit.

The Village Development Boards are bringing the planning process to grass root level. However, they are facing some practical difficulties, which are given below:

a) Due to thin distributions of horticulture and animal husbandry schemes, it is not possible to generate an affective delivery system of goods and services to help the effective running of the schemes. As the production is meagre it is not possible to create a viable marketing channel.

b) In absence of the defined criteria, the identification of the beneficiaries in poverty alleviation programmes becomes difficult, leading to a tendency to include too many persons in the category of 'poor' resulting into this distribution of resources. Thus in most of the cases the scheme becomes ineffective.

c) The assistance under the present schemes is given only once. As a result, often there are cases of relapse of the gains. There is a need of repeated assistance.

d) The subsidy in many poverty alleviation programmes is lower than that under general sector schemes.

e) Paucity of technical personnel also brings difficulty in the implementation of the schemes.

It is also observed that there is multiplicity of programmes and overlapping activities of the agencies. This decreases the effectivity of rural development programmes.

The village forests have adequate potential for the growth of the area. There is enormous scope of development of social forestry in the tribal areas of the North-East. However, the government has to genuinely convince the villagers that it does not want to grab their land and forests. Without bridging such a communication gap between the government and people, it is not possible to properly utilise and mobilise this vast resource.

The tribal polity in North East is diverse in nature. The chang polity was democratic in nature with some social disabilities for women and adopted (Bumbti) section of the society. They followed some sort of chieftainship, but their chiefs were powerless in comparison to Kukamis (Sema chiefs) and Angs (Konyak chiefs). In practice, their chieftainship was symbolic rather than functionary in nature.

Every village in olden days was just like a republic with elaborate self defence arrangements. Sometimes two or more sections (Khels) of the village also had their separate defence arrangement and worked as separate political units.

The administrative and judicial powers in the past were vested in the Village Council consisting of the village chief (the founder of the village), the priest and the councillers i.e., village elders representing different clans. The adopted clan members had to conform to the wishes of the adopter class. The practice of adult franchise has now eliminated such disability.

The British tried to reorganize the traditional village leadership and appointed the chief as *Head Gaon Burhas* (GBs) and village elders as *Barika* and tried to rule the villages through them. They also appointed the interpreters (Debhashis or DBs), who not only conveyed government standing orders to the villagers but also interpreted intricate and controversial customary laws and thus became valuable guides in the task of enforcing the judicial administration in its correct perspective. This gradually developed into the establishment of Debhashi Courts. Thus for the first time in their area, an agency was established whose authority extended over an area of more than a village. This also led to the dilution of powers of the village authority. DBs were given superior powers than GBs. The channel of appeal against the GBs decision was to the DB and then to the Sub-Divisional Officer/Deputy Commissioner and finally to the High Court.

The evolution of the three tier local self government started soon after the establishment of a systematic administration. Initially, Village Councils, Range Councils and Tribal Councils were established in 1961-62 under article 13 of Nagaland Regulation. The Village Councils consisted of the recognised Chief or Chiefs, *Gaon Burhas* and the elders elected by the village in accordance with the customary procedures, being responsible for matters relating to the internal administration of the village and the organisation of welfare works and enforcement of all orders, rules and regulation passed by the legal authorities including the maintenance of law and order. The Range and Tribal Councils had overriding powers over that of the village councils. In Tuensang district, there was also a district council with enormous powers given under the Nagaland Act even to elect members of the state legislatures.

Further reorganisation of the Councils as per Nagaland Village and Area Council Act 1978, resulted in the reconstitution of Village and Area councils. The village Development Boards were formed in the village under Section 58 of the above mentioned Act. These Boards function as the wing of the village councils under their guidance and are made responsible for village level development works.

Traditional factors like being a member of the founder's family or of a dominant clan, personal success in head-hunting or in giving feasts of merit heavily influenced the selection of candidates in the Village Councils in the past. While the family background still helps a candidate in such matters the success war and feasts have lost weightage. New personal factors like educational background, link with people in power at the district or state levels and the capacity to get things done, capacity to spend money during elections have emerged as new factors in the selection of political elites. These new factors have overriding influence on earlier social disabilities and at a time cause short lived social tension. However, people are fast learning to conform to the realities of the changing situation.

The Nagas are a very hard working people, and spend their leisure in festivals songs and dances, games and sports. War and head hunting was another activity in the past which has been stopped and is still remembered nostalgically by the old people.

Most of the Naga festivals were agricultural in nature and were held during slack agricultural seasons. In the beginning, the new Christian converts thought them to be the part of the heathen religion and practices and tended to dissociate from them. However, they started to realise the importance of such festivals very soon. Nowadays Naga festivals are celebrated by Christians and non-Christians alike.

The Nagas, before the advent Christianity followed their age-old animist religion. Their old faith was a way of life for them which included their polytheistic faith in gods, spirits, souls and ghosts, their history, traditions, beliefs, superstitions and mode of worship. Their religion and social life were intertwined. Songs were sung in praise of the warriors and generous givers of feasts during religious festivals. Life after death was visualised as replica of life in this world.

The Naga language, according to Grierson, belongs

to the Naga group of the Assam-Burmese branch of the Tibeto-Burmese sub-family of the Tibeto-Chinese family of languages. After Grierson, only two persons, namely R. Shafer and Marrison have studied this language. They do not have their own script and writing is done in Roman script nowadays.

Nagamese like elsewhere in Nagaland, has become the *lingua frnca* in the Naga area, though Hindi, and English are also widely used.

The dialect used for Bible translation, such as Chougli in Ao become a dialect. Christian missionaries adopted the four dialects of the Chang language for the translation of the Tuensang dialect out of the Gospels and the Bible. As a result the language is very rapidly assuming the position of the standard dialect. The same dialect is used by Text-Book Production Branch of the Education Directorate of the Nagaland Government for the preparation of school text books.

Practically the only published literature except for half a dozen other books in every language, consists of Christian literature and a few school textbooks. The vast oral literature is not yet collected, compiled and published. Creative writing has not yet started.

The Naga way of life remained unchanged for centuries practically upto the beginning of this century. The winds of change started blowing some half century ago, and with rapidity after the attainment of statehood. Today there is no aspect of their life and culture-political, economic, religious, social and linguistic- which remains untouched by change and which has not passed through the phases of transition and transformation. They are no more insulated from outside influence any more.

The changes in the material culture- like the use of lanterns; lamps, matches, battery, torches, electric elements, shoes, umbrellas, utensils, modern western dress, cosmetics, watches, modern furniture, guns- have taken place practically in every village. Their food habits have changed. Milk did not remain a taboo. Tea, biscuits, pulses, *chapati*, new fruits and vegetables, tinned food-stuff, silently entered their kitchen.

In the changed circumstances, when there was no fear of war and violence, it no more remained necessary to construct houses in well protected boundaries of congested villages. Many persons preferred to build modern houses by the road side with corrugated sheet roofings, lime washed walls and ceilings, well ventilated doors and windows, stilts, electrification and modern furnitures. They have modern tiolets in their houses and no more go to the nearby forests for nature's call. Thus a large number of households have achieved an all-together new standard of living and a high index of socio-economic transformation.

The main factors which brought socio-economic change in their society - modern education, Christianity, administration, monetary economy and urbanization- emerged almost together at least in the Tuensang area. The attitude towards education was not the same every where, for example education was not accepted readily by the dominant sections of the Chang population. They were afraid that by their absence from the village, they would lose control over their lands. A saying most common in those days was that "Only the lazy persons go to the schools". However, it did not take much time for them to realise the material gain of the education and they developed the feeling of lagging behind and a sense of urgency and competition for education.

The Nagas from the very beginning considered education as something which made them fit for "sitting and eating jobs", the jobs carrying status but not involving manual labour. Education led to "no work" ethos and therefore an escape from strict village discipline and manual labour and as a result, even the drop-outs do not return to villages to pursue the old way of life. Christianity faced stiff opposition from village Chiefs and priests. However, as the early Christians were also the persons who received education first and got white collar jobs, they soon found themselves highly placed in comparison to the traditional village elites. This brought about a change in their attitude towards Christianity. Moreover, most of the Naga leaders, ministers, government officers etc. were Christians and this had its due psychological impact. The fear of hell-fire, substitution of a set of taboos by another, loosening grip of the old value system etc. also helped in the process of conversion.

Christian missionaries contributed much in the field of education, public health, provided them scripts and standard dialects etc. However, their wholesale rejection of Naga culture resulting in virtual abolition of such ideal institutions as *Morung* is regrettable. Christianity also adversely affected their folk-songs, folk-tales, dances, dress, festivals etc. and highly undermined the importance of the traditional religious and magical experts.

The sense of superiority among average school and college goers in an unlettered or first generation educated society is not uncommon. The sense of superiority coupled with Christianity contributed to undermining the importance of traditional leadership. Education and Christianity both undermined the importance of the clan and village authority and made every person conscious of his/her individuality and rights. Administration and law also recognised individual's rights. Thus it was not difficult for every individual to place his/her own interest over those of the clan and openly challenge its authority. As a result, there is disintegration and indiscipline and spirit of sacrifice and unity has disappeared.

The government efforts in putting an end to the violence, as well as its efforts at all round development and modernization are welcomed every where. However, it has created a psychological problem, the problem of highly increased expectation from the government that it should do everything for the people. This is killing their initiative and work ethos.

As a result of the huge money pumped in by the government for administration and development, readily available white collar jobs and increased opportunity to earn cash by daily wage earning, the barter economy, though not completely removed, gave way to cash economy. There was money to facilitate opening of markets, which brought rapid change in their material culture.

The changes brought about by the various factors mentioned above have varied and often overlapping effects. Upsurge of aspirations, growth of individualism, weakening of clan and village ties, urge of delinking them from the past, consumerism, no work ethos, removal of social disabilities and widenning gap between rich and poor are some of the main changes brought about by these factors. Of late, they are becoming conscious of their culture and the Christians and non-Christians alike have started participating in the Chang festivals.

By adopting western dress, Christianity, and the English language, they are getting westernized; though it is the westernization without western technology.

As a result of the huge money spent by the government for administration and development, readily available white collar jobs and increased opportunity to earn cash by daily wage labour, the barter economy though not completely removed, gave way [illegible] there was money to facilitate opening of markets, which brought rapid change in their material culture.

The changes brought about by the various factors mentioned above have varied and [illegible] pattern of settlements, growth of [illegible] [illegible] of their villages, [illegible] them from the [illegible] work [illegible] removed [illegible] disabilities and widening gap between rich and poor are some of the main changes brought about by these factors. [illegible] they are becoming conscious of their [illegible] have also have started participating in the [illegible] system.

[illegible] adopting western dress, Christianity, and the English language they are [illegible] though it is the westernisation [illegible] western technology.

Index